CONVERSATIONS WITH MILLIONAIRES

What Millionaires Do To Get Rich, That You Never Learned About In School!

Mike Litman

Jason Oman

Conversations with Millionaires is a trademark of Michael Litman and Jason Oman

Chicken Soup for the Soul is a trademark of Chicken Soup Enterprises, Inc.
1-800-FLOWERS and 1-800-FLOWERS.com are trademarks of 1-800-FLOWERS.com, Inc.
Cashflow Quadrant is a trademark of Cashflow Technologies, Inc.

This publication is designed to provide competent and reliable information regarding the subject matters covered. However, it is sold with the understanding that the authors and publisher are not engaged in rendering legal, financial, or other professional advice. Laws and practices often vary from state to state and if legal or other expert assistance is required, the services of a professional should be sought. The authors and publisher specifically disclaim any liability that is incurred from the use or application of the contents of this book.

Visit our website at: www.cwmbook.com

Printed in the United States of America

ISBN 1-931866-007

Book Designed by Jason Oman

Get Two Valuable FREE Gifts At: www.cwmbook.com

FREE! - Two Special Bonus Gifts

As our way of saying *thank you* for taking an active role in your success education, we have made two additional bonus gifts available to you. They are each worth $19.95, and are yours free as a reader of Conversations with Millionaires.

All you have to do to get your bonus gifts is visit our special website at: www.cwmbook.com and the gifts are yours free. Thank you and enjoy reading.

This book is dedicated to all the individuals who want the most that life has to offer.
We sincerely hope this book helps you
Make Your Move.

What People Are Saying About
Conversations with Millionaires...

"Awesome! A fiery, practical, inspiring and informative powerhouse collection! Mike is a fire-breathing interviewer who pulls the gold out of the gurus. Get this book! It's fantastic!"

> **Joe "Mr. Fire" Vitale**, author of "Spiritual Marketing,"
> www.mrfire.com

"Mike Litman is one of the most exciting young people of our time dedicated to helping others find their true potential and ultimately SUCCESS. If you read his book *Conversations with Millionaires* you will see for yourself that it is not wishful thinking to become a happy, balanced and rich human being. These interviews with successful people show us how they did it. It does not matter what your background or education read this book and you too can become a Millionaire and someone you can be proud of. Thank you Mike"

> **Michele Blood**, inventor of MusiVation, co-author of
> "Be A Magnet To Money", www.musivation.com

"*Conversations with Millionaires* is pure wisdom straight from the people who achieved what you are shooting for: The goal of becoming a millionaire! While other books tout theory, *Conversations with Millionaires* gives you truths from people who have actually done it. You won't find better information or advice anywhere!"

> **Chris Widener**, President,
> www.MadeForSuccess.com

"Mike, you have performed a great service to those individuals who are sincerely seeking true personal, spiritual and financial freedom!"

> **Rick Beneteau**, Author of the best-selling,
> Ezine Marketing Machine, www.interniche.net

"When I read *Conversations with Millionaires*, I was floored. The people in this book understand the principals behind achievement and are masters at transferring that knowledge so anyone can duplicate it. Mike's ability to draw out just the jewels from these titans is amazing. It's like he was reading their minds. Get this book! Read it over and over. It'll be worth thousands, and maybe millions to the fortunate people who own it."

Mike Brescia, President of Think Right Now Publishing
www.thinkrightnow.com

"It was with awe that I finished reading Mike's book, *Conversations with Millionaires*. Found in one volume is the amazing, simple secrets to wealth, success and happiness told by some of the most remarkable people on Earth. If you read one book this month, make sure this is it."

John Harricharan, best-selling author of,
"When You Can Walk on Water, Take the Boat"
www.powerpause.com

"If you're interested in gaining insight from today's greatest leaders in the areas of personal growth and development, this is a must read!"

Liz Randazzese, EmpowerX! Seminar coach

"*Conversations with Millionaires* is absolutely Fantastic. I have no doubt that you'll be creating many more millionaires with this. Most people want to become a millionaire but haven't been shown what these rich people do to get there until now...Great Job."

Jerome Chapman, Creator of 1hourwealth.com

2

ACKNOWLEDGEMENTS:

W e'd like to thank a host of people for helping us take this project from the invisible to the visible. First we'd like to thank Mark Victor Hansen and Jack Canfield. Through their writings, both of these extraordinary individuals taught us to think larger, think about others, and were part of the inspiration behind the *Conversations with Millionaires* series.

Mike would especially like to thank Les Brown for reminding him that it takes real courage to live your dreams and for helping to bring that realization to life over the past years. Wally 'Famous' Amos because when Mike met him a few years ago, looking at him instilled in Mike the belief that staying upbeat and genuine pays off in the long run for yourself and everybody around you. Sharon Lechter and Robert Kiyosaki because they shared the education of financial literacy to both of us and enabled us to see a path where financial freedom can be gained. Jim McCann has shown all of us that with a passion, a dream, and determination, there is nothing we cannot do. To Michael Gerber because when meeting him and listening to his message he taught us how to own a business and not own a job.

We'd like to thank all of the mentors of the individuals mentioned above. Without their patience, insight, and delight in giving, our dream of bringing this book to the world could never have been realized.

Mike would also like to give a special thanks to Jason Oman, because it was his big thinking that inspired the idea behind the *Conversation with Millionaires* series. Without Jason's idea, the great information inside would not have been shared with the world in this format.

Jason would also like to give special thanks to Robert Allen for being the incredible mentor he is and also Denise Michaels for being such an angel. Jason would also like to thank his mother, Merry Oman, and also all of the mentors who have created the success path Jason now follows.

Mike also sends a big thank you to Trudy Marschall, Ken Young, Teresa Esparza, Karen Boga, and Kyle Wilson for all their assistance in this project.

Plus, Mike also sends thanks to a few very important people in his life: "Shawn Cantor, Andrew Leibman, Ken Stein, and Charlie Dankner for always believing in my projects. My awesome girlfriend Marcie Glick for her unwavering support and incredible smile. My grandparents Rita Litman and Bertha Krissoff for their constant love. Most importantly, to my Mom, Dad, and brother who somehow believed in me when I was in 'muddy waters' and who encourage me as I share this message."

To all, gratitude into eternity.

Mike Litman
& Jason Oman

Contents

Worldwide Success Mentor to Millions of People
Success Principles That Never Fail
Defining Ultimate Success...A Principle That Can Change Your
Destiny...Improve This and You'll Change Your Life...How To
Get The Pay You Desire...Getting Started Towards Financial
Independence...The Choice That Leads To Fortune...The "Fork"
of Financial Freedom...He Worked 'On Himself' And Made His
Family A Fortune...Double, Triple, Or Even Quadruple Your
Income, Here's How...Sometimes It's About Your Business
Philosophy...From Broke To Millionaire In 6 Years...Organizing
Your Time Like the Rich and Famous

Co-Author of Chicken Soup for the Soul Book Series
Secrets to Unlimited Riches
How To Start Thinking With Prosperity Consciousness... The
Power of Human Imagination...How To Think Like a Billionaire...
The 4 Keys To Prosperity...A Little-Known Miracle Method for
Getting Whatever You Need ...Solving Problems In Just Minutes...
Simple Four Step Success Plan...A Unique Approach to the Idea of
Goal-Setting...A Powerful Lesson from Walt Disney...The
Decision That Made the Difference... A Morning Ritual That
Creates The Perfect Day...Two Tactics for Tapping into Treasure...
How an "Accident" Created a Millionaire...Ideas Become Fortunes

Get Two Valuable FREE Gifts At: www.cwmbook.com

Turning Your Passion Into Profit
How His Ideas Became A Reality...A Setback Is A Setup For A
Comeback...The #1 Mistake Of The Entrepreneur...The Core
Principle Of Total Life Success...The Passion Behind The Idea...
The Day I Began To Listen...How I Visualized My Success

Develop Unlimited Self-Esteem and the Riches That Come With It
The Power of The 'Hidden' Success Factor...Simple Steps for
Increasing Your Self-Esteem...The Creative Businessman Who
Made a Fortune...The Best-Kept Secret of the Rich...The Ultimate
Universal Truth...Two Breakthroughs for Breaking the Bank...A
Common Missing Ingredient for Success

Secrets for Creating Multiple Streams of Income!
The Secret to Financial Freedom in Today's World...Six Ways to
Make Money While You Sleep...The Most Powerful Money
Force...The Path That Leads to Wealth...Seven Essential Money
Skills of Millionaires...The Critical Factor for Long-Term
Wealth...Three Required Skills for Wealth...An Unknown
Characteristic of Millionaires...The Ultimate Key to Online Riches

*How To Invent Money / How Rich Dad's Recipe Can Make You
Financially Free for Life*
A "Drop Out" Who Made a Fortune...Your Financial Report
Card...The Three Types of Income...The Biggest Secret of the
Rich...A Million Dollar Lesson You Must Learn...The Millionaire
Mindset...The Smart Way To Buy Luxuries...The First Step to
Financial Freedom

Systems: The Key to Wealth and Freedom
The Myth That Kills Small Businesses...The Real Purpose of Creating a Business...The Incident That Changed the Business World ...A Concept That Can Transform Any Business... The Real Work of a Business Owner...An Important Key to Business Success...The Foundation of Your Business... How Ordinary People Can Create Extra-Ordinary Results...The "Routine" Mistake of Failing Entrepreneurs...How To Turn Your Business Into A Winner

How To Build An Empire
The Surprising Story of a Local Florist...From Failure to Fortune...A Semi-Commandment for Success...Ideas Don't Have To Be "Sexy" To Be Successful...A Secret Ingredient of Millionaires...Try This Technique Before Getting Into Business...The Power of "The Contact Economy"

How To Master the Art of Guerrilla Marketing
Four Different Ways to Make an Absolute Fortune...Guerrilla marketing vs. traditional marketing...The guerrilla marketer's only concern...Reaching your prospect's subconscious mind...An option you can't pass up...Because I stayed in touch...How to ask to always receive...The cost of ignorance...Reaching more prospects without cost...A twelve month plan laid out for you... Taking your prospect from apathy to excitement

Get Two Valuable FREE Gifts At: www.cwmbook.com

FOREWORD

Over the years I've been asked on many occasions, "What can I do to make more money and become wealthy?" This has probably been the most asked question of me throughout my twenty plus year career.

My three New York Times Best Selling books: *Nothing Down, Creating Wealth, Multiple Streams of Income,* and soon *Multiple Streams of Internet Income* each go into many of the specifics to reaching that goal. But, there is something I always say to the person who asks me that very question.

The answer to the question I mentioned earlier is as follows. 'How do you get started on the road to success?' The answer is, *learn from those who have already paved the path to riches and fortune.* Learn from those who have generated the grand ideas, laid out the vision, assembled a plan, and fought the adversities that lay ahead of any great success story. Learn from those who have dropped the success clues along the way.

In these days of the Internet, information is everywhere. Getting information is easy. Though getting great information is tough and often very challenging.

In *Conversations with Millionaires,* you'll get life changing information from some of the most successful entrepreneurs in America today. All in one book, all at one time.

This is a book I wish I had 20 years ago when I started on my own journey to become a millionaire.

Although I didn't have this book back then, I view it as a treasure today for all those who are striving for more in their lives.

Whether you are looking for greater prosperity, greater wealth, or greater happiness, this book can assist you.

As I read the radio interviews that Mike Litman has compiled throughout the years, dare I even say, including my own, I'm taken aback by the incredible information his guests have shared. You can almost feel their passion flowing off the pages as you turn them. Almost like you're in the radio studio, listening in on their live interview. How fortunate we are that this information has been shared in another form.

Conversations with Millionaires is not only a book, but also a guide for those looking to achieve more abundance and riches in their life.

As I said, success leaves clues, you'll discover them as you turn the pages in this soon-to-be business classic.

Robert Allen -
NY Times Best-Selling Author of:
Nothing Down, Creating Wealth, and
Multiple Streams of Income

Sometimes, as they say, truth is stranger than fiction.

This story falls into that same category. It's the story of how the "Conversations with Millionaires" phenomenon began.

It happened to two friends living on opposite sides of the country. One in New York. One in California. Each holding nothing. Nothing ....but a dream.

They had both gone the usual path. They went to school, received their degrees, and then did what so many others do. They went from job to job, job to job.

"Get good grades, go to college, get a job." We're told it's all great from there. Sound familiar? It's the pattern many of us are taught.

Months and years of unsatisfying work. They met with a little 'success'. But, a lot more failure. More than that though, they were flat-out unfulfilled. They were leading lives of 'quiet desperation' as Henry David Thoreau once called it.

This story would sound like so many before it, except for one thing. The one thing that would later go on to change thousands of lives.

You see each of them had a glimpse of the world they so desperately wanted. One of happiness, riches, and success.

Luckily, on a tiny local radio station in the suburbs of Long Island, New York one of them would do a weekly one-hour radio show interviewing some of the most successful people alive.

Individuals of all ages, races, and creeds who had accomplished extraordinary things.

It was with this opportunity that 'Mike' was afforded the unique opportunity to ask millionaires any questions he wanted on improving one's life and improving one's business.

At this same time in California something else was happening.

A long distance call was being placed.

Mike's friend Jason, though in California, was never far away.

Why?

Because each week when the show would broadcast, Jason would call across the country and ask to be put on hold at the radio station so he could hear the entire radio show.

There he could 'listen in' on the millionaire interviews and get all the success strategies revealed by the guest.

In a world of confusion, fear, and more, once a week they were able to zero in on where they wanted to go. Once a week the strategies, tips, and techniques of America's most successful entrepreneurs were being revealed right into their 'ears'.

As time went on, they'd found themselves reviewing past shows and then looking forward to the next exciting guest coming on. They were using the information revealed in these interviews as a roadmap for their own lives. For their own success.

You see, these conversations gave them the game plan they need-ed to design their goals and go for their dreams. And it changed their lives forever.

It was then that Jason had the idea to put all of these life-changing interviews into a book and call it "Conversations with Millionaires".

Inside this book, you'll be given the same life-changing opportu-nity Mike and Jason received. An opportunity to 'listen in' to those same 'Conversations with Millionaires'.

Chapter One

Conversation with Jim Rohn

(Introduction)

Over the last 38 years, spanning almost four decades, this individual has influenced people that have trained a whole class of personal development students. People like Mark Victor Hansen, Anthony Robbins, and more.

IIe's the author of dozens of books and cassettes, courses on success, on living a life that is your potential, and realizing your dreams.

Tonight, I will bring to you, the one, the only, Jim Rohn. Author of many books I've talked about.

Tonight we're going to go A to Z on how you can live a life of success in business and in family. How do you do that?

Why is he the mentor for millions of people worldwide?

(To Jim)

Jim Rohn, my dime, your dance floor.
Welcome to *The Mike Litman Show*.

Hey, thanks Mike. I'm happy to be here.

Great. I know myself and everyone is very excited for you to share some wisdom tonight and talk about the concept of success and about the principles for achieving it in our next 57 minutes together.

I'd like to start out by defining the word.
What is being a success?

What does success mean to Jim Rohn?

Well, I think the ultimate success, which I teach in my seminar, is living a good life.

Part of it is income. Part of it's financial independence Part of it is objectives that you achieve, dreams coming true, family, children, grandchildren, good friends, productivity. It's a wide range.

It's all encompassing, the word "success".

It's not just your job, your income, your fortune. Not just your paycheck or your bank account. But everything. From all of your achievements during your life to trying your best to design a way to make it all give you a good life.

So, we're talk about design.

We'll get to ambition.

We're talking about goals. We're talking about planning.

You talk about something in your literature.

You mention that success doesn't need to be pursued. It needs to be attracted.

What do you mean by that?

That's true.

I was taught, starting at age 25. when I met a mentor of mine by the name of Mr. Schoff.

He taught me that success is something you attract by the person you become.

You've got to develop the skills.

He talked about personal development: become a good communicator, learn to use your own language.

He talked about the management of time.

But primarily developing yourself, your attitude, your personality, developing your own character, your reputation. Then developing the skills. From sales skills to recruiting skills, to management skills, leadership skills, how to work with a variety of people. You know, the full list.

He taught me to work on myself, because I used to work on my job.

He said, "if you work on yourself, you can make a fortune."

That turned out to be true for me.

He turned it all around and said, "success is not something you run after, like a better job." Although that is to be desired.

You've just got to ask yourself, "am I qualified for doubling, tripling, multiplying my income by three, four, five?"

If I look at myself and say, "No, not really." Then I need to ask myself, "Who could I find? Where can I go that could pay me three, four, five times as much money?"

Then, you have to say, "at the present there probably isn't anyone. I can't just fall into a lucky deal."

But, if I went to work on myself immediately. Work on my attitude, personality, language, and skills. Then that begins the process of attracting the good job, the good people, and building a business or creating a career that could turn out to make you financially independent, perhaps wealthy.

Jim, so really what we are talking about is a change of mindset. Of changing our thinking and getting in tune with the universe.

Talk about something that you mentioned. Changing your language.

Describe what that means.

There is the language that can fit.

You can use careless language around home and around the community.

But, if you want to start stepping up, then you've got to learn the language. The corporate language. You've got to learn the sales language.

Then you've got to be careful not to be careless with your language in the marketplace. It can cost you too much.

You know, a guy that is inclined to tell dirty stories, inclined to use a bit too much profanity.

It might be okay in the inner circle and at the bar or whatever. But when you start to move into the world of business and finance where you want to be successful, earn a better paycheck, move up the scale, you just have to be careful. So, one of the major things is your language.

Not just that, but learning the language of success. Learning how to treat people with respect. Giving people inspiration when they need it, correction when they need it.

The same thing as learning to work with your children.

Language opens the door for fortune. It opens the door for help. It opens the door for better living. It opens the door for a good marriage. It opens the door for a stable friendship.

A big part of it starts with our thinking, our attitude, and then a major part of it is the language we use.

Okay, something that we are sharing tonight with people worldwide now, is we are talking about an inner change, then the outer result.

So many times people are trying to change the outer, without changing the inner. Is that what we are talking about?

Yeah, that's true.

The big part of it, of course, is to start with philosophy.

Making mistakes and judgements can just cost you so much in the marketplace, at home, with your family, whatever it is. Errors in judgement can really do us in. It can leave us with less of a life than we could've had.

We've got to learn to correct those errors whether they are errors in philosophy or something else.

My mentor asked once why I wasn't doing well.

I showed him my paycheck and I said, "This is all the company pays." He said, "well, that's really not true. With that philosophy, you'll never grow."

I said, "No, no, this *is* my paycheck. This is all the company pays." So, he said, "No, no, Mr. Rohn. This is all that the company pays *you*."

I thought, 'wow, I'd never thought about that.'

He said, "doesn't the company pay some people two, three, four five times this amount?" I said, "well yes." He said, "then this is not all that the company pays. This is all

20

that the company pays you."

For your income to multiple by three, four, five, you can't say to the company, "I need more money." You've just got to say to yourself, 'I need a correction in my philosophy. I can't blame circumstance. I can't blame taxes. I can't say it's too far, too hot, too cold. I've got to come to grips with myself.'

That is really where it all begins. It's corrections of errors in judgement and in your own philosophy.

We're talking about philosophy. Is it really like ironing down a purpose?

You're talking about the word "philosophy" to someone listening right now and they're trying to put it into actual practice.

Someone right now that's in a rut, lost, how do you go about the process of putting together a philosophy that excites you and that benefits others?

You start with the easy stuff.

Ask most people, "what is your current philosophy for financial independence that you're now working on?", and usually the person says, "Gosh, I never thought about that."

Unless you have an excellent financial philosophy that gives you guidance to correct errors, accept some new disciplines, and make some changes, you can forget being financially independent.

Ask yourself, "What is your philosophy on good health?" Is it to cross your fingers and sort of let it go and if something goes wrong *then* you fix it?

The answer is, no. You should try to learn up front.

Ask yourself, "what is your cholesterol count?" The average guy's philosophy is, 'I don't know and I don't care. If something goes wrong, I will try to fix it.'

But, by then usually it's too late. Now it'll cost you a fortune. It costs you time. Maybe even it costs you your life.

If someone can help you with errors in judgement, or help you correct your financial philosophy, your spiritual philosophy, your philosophy on a good relationship, that's where it all begins.

21

We go the direction we face, and we face the direction we think.

It's the things we think about and ponder. What are your values? What's good? What's not so good? What's the better way? What's the best way?

Unless we do some constructive thinking on that, we usually take the easier way.

Easy causes drift, and drift causes us to arrive at a poor destination a year or five years from now.

So, we're talking about increasing our self-awareness. We're talking about philosophy.

I want to transition to a concept of planning, but before I do, Jim, let's talk about something you have been talking about for decades.

You give people options and you give people a choice.

You say, "you can either be in somebody else's plan or playing in your own life." Can you talk about that?

That's true. Some people sort of resign to letting somebody else create the productivity, create the business, create the job, and it seems to be easier for them to punch the clock and let everyone else have the responsibility. Then they go home and try to make the best of it.

But, I think it is also good to start pondering and thinking, 'how could I take charge of my own life? Or whether I qualify for a better position where I am. Or whether I might create my own business, start something, developing from my personal productivity.'

If we just sit back and not take responsibility, that is what happens. Then we fit into someone else's plans, rather than designing plans of our own.

If you don't have plans of your own to fill that vacuum, you're probably going to fit into someone else's plan.

Jim, what if you don't know what the plan is?

What happens to someone when they're at a job right now, 9 to 5, working the clock, they don't know what they're passionate about, they don't know where to go, where do they start?

You don't have to operate from passion to begin with. You operate from necessity.

My friend, Bill Bailey, said when he got out of high school he went to Chicago from Kentucky and the first job he could find was night janitor.

Someone asked him, "how come you settled for a job as night janitor?" He said, "malnutrition."

So, the first passion is to survive. To somehow make it.

Then start to build from there with something that you could find to do even if it is distasteful.

You don't have to love what you do. Just love the chance or the opportunity to begin the process. Because where you begin is not where you have to end a year from now, five years from now, ten years from now.

You just begin, first of all, to correct errors.

Find something, anything, it doesn't matter what.

America is such an incredible country especially. The ladder of success is available for everybody.

If you have to start at the bottom and make your way to the top, who cares? As long as they let you on the ladder.

Then, if you study, and grow, and learn, and take classes, and read books, burn a little midnight oil, start investing some of your own ambition, I'm telling you, the changes can be absolutely dramatic.

That is what happened for me starting age 25.

At age 25, in a six-year period, you went from being broke to becoming a millionaire.

Obviously, you put this stuff into practice. You started your own, I'll use the words, "mental make over", changing your thoughts, changing your attitude.

It seems to me, and this is personal for me, Jim, this quote of yours influences me tremendously even today, "discipline versus regret."

23

Talk about the importance of that. Talk about how to live a disciplined life and stay disciplined so you can get what you want.

It is true. We suffer one of two things. Either the pain of discipline or the pain of regret.

You've got to choose discipline, versus regret, because discipline weighs ounces and regret weighs tons.

Say that again.

Discipline weighs ounces and regret weighs tons.
The reason is because the regret is an accumulated affect a year from now, two years from now. When you didn't do the easy discipline.

It's like having a cavity in your tooth. The dentist says, "if we fix it now it's only $300, and if you let it go someday it's going to be $3,000."

So, the easier pain of the $300 and sitting in the chair for just a little while takes care of it. But, if you let it go that's no good.

You know, the dentist says, "this cavity is not going to get better by itself. This is something you have got to take care of. You can't cross your fingers and hope it's going to go away. That's not going to help."

Whatever you see that needs to be corrected, you start taking care of it.

If you don't have a splendid diet, you've got to be incredibly thoughtful about how to change that.

If your kids don't have a splendid diet, you've got to say, "hey, maybe I should give some attention to my kids and their diet."

Nutrition affects behavior I was taught at age 25. Nutrition affects learning. Nutrition affects performance. Nutrition affects vitality. Nutrition affects decision making. Nutrition affects longevity.

My mother studied and practiced good nutrition and talked to me about it, an only child, and my father too, who lived to be 93.

24

The doctor told me that my mother extended her life at least 20 years by paying attention to nutrition and practicing the art.

The benefits are so incredible by taking a look at a few simple disciplines.

You know, if mom said, 'an apple a day', and the guy says, 'well, no. I'm not into the apple a day, I've got my fingers crossed and I think everything is going to be okay.', you've just got to say, 'this is a foolish person.'

It doesn't matter what it is. You don't have to take giant steps at first.

To have an incredible increase in self-esteem, all you have to do is start doing some little something. Whether it is to benefit your health, benefit your marriage, or to benefit your business, or your career.

You can eat the first apple of the new apple a day philosophy along with some other things you have decided to do. You could say one of these days I will never be healed again. I'm going to have all the breath I need. I'm going to have all the vitality I need. I'm munching on the first apple.

You don't have to revolutionize all at once. Just start.

But, the first apple you eat, if it's a plan to better health, I'm telling you, by the end of that first day your self-esteem starts to grow.

Say to yourself, 'I promise myself I'll never be the same again.'

It doesn't take a revolution. You don't have to do spectacularly dramatic things for self-esteem to start going off the scale. Just make a commitment to any easy discipline. Then another one and another one.

It doesn't take but just a collection of those new easy disciplines to start giving you the idea that you're going to change every part of your life: financial, spiritual, social.

A year from now, you'll be almost unrecognizable as the mediocre person you may have been up until now. All of that can change.

It doesn't change over night. But, it does change with a change in thought and philosophy.

Pick up a new discipline and start it immediately.

When you bring up action, like Jack Canfield on the show awhile ago talking about the universe rewards action, we talked about the concept of doing it personally. We can both concur on this, amazing things happen.

Those little baby steps create momentum. They create energy, force, and they create something that I want to steer back to.

You talk a lot about ambition, the fuel of achievement.

You talk about being ambitious.

I personally saw my life revolutionized when I found something that I enjoyed and made it a necessity to be ambitious about it.

Talk about the power of ambition. How do we build a life where we become ambitious?

Sometimes ambition just lingers below the surface. All of the possibilities for ambition are there.

But, if you live an undisciplined life drifting on health, drifting on relationships, drifting on developing a better career, if you're drifting, it doesn't taste good at the end of the day. But, if you start something, I promise you, not only will you feel better about yourself in terms of self esteem, which develops self confidence, which is one of the greatest things in stepping towards success, it'll also start awakening a spark of ambition.

A person who has never sold anything in their life. Finally they get a product they can believe in. They make the first sale and all of a sudden they say, "gosh, if I did this once, I can do it again."

By the time they've made the 10th sale they say, "this could be the career for me. It could be the steps I need to become a leader. To become a giant in my field."

All of that stuff has the potential of awakening your ambition. To make the flames start to burn. It starts to grow.

But, it just doesn't grow unless you start the process.

You can't just say, "I'm praying and hoping that ambition will cease me tomorrow morning and everything will change."

Just start with some little something to prove to yourself that you're going to develop a whole list of disciplines.

Start with the easy ones first. It doesn't matter. Like making the necessary contacts in whatever business you're in.

If you make three phone calls a day, in a year that's *a thousand.*

Three does not sound like much. But, in a year it's a thousand.

If you make three positive calls a day, if you make a thousand positive calls, something *phenomenal* is going to happen to your life.

I also teach that the things that are easy to do are easy not to do.

If you want to learn a new language, three words a day, at the end of the year it gives you a vocabulary of a thousand words.

It's just easy *to*, but it's easy *not* to.

It's easier to hope it will get better than to start the process of making it better.

That is really the theme of my seminars.

(To the listeners)

On the topic of seminars, go to jimrohn.com to find out more about Jim's seminars.

When you go to jimrohn.com subscribe to his newsletter.

There are tons of people that Jim has influenced and you'll hear the information tonight.

(Back to Jim)

Talk about the power, simplicity, and importance of having strong reasons.

That's major. If you have enough reasons, you can do anything.

If you have enough reasons, you'll read all the books you need to read.

If you have enough reasons, enough goals, enough objectives, enough things that you want to accomplish in your life, you'll attend whatever classes you need to attend. You'll get up however early you need to get up.

Sometimes we find it a little hard to get out of bed. We want to linger. Part of that is not just being tired, or weary, or a little bit of poor nutrition, some of it is just lack of the drive in terms of having a long enough list of reasons to do it.

Then you've just got to let the reasons grow. Things you thought were important this year, you go for them, then next year you look back and you say, "I was a little foolish about that. Here's what I really want. That isn't really important to me anymore." Then you just keep up this process of what's important to you.

For your family, build a financial wall around your family nothing can get through.

I made that statement, about six years ago, to a young couple that have twins.

Fabulous. They now earn about five to six million dollars a year.

I remember the day they came to me and said, "you know that statement you made about building a financial wall around your family that nothing can get through? Well, we resolved to do that. Now we're happy to report to you that we have just crossed the line. We have now finished building the financial wall around our family nothing can get through."

I'm telling you, the power of something like that is amazing. That's just a small example of all the things that can inspire your life.

Where do you want to go? Who do you want to meet? How many skills do you want to learn this year? How many languages do you want to learn?

I go and lecture in the Scandinavian countries. They all speak four or five, six languages. In the school system you are required to learn four languages. Three they assign, and one you can pick.

I mean, there isn't anything you can't do in terms of language, skills, business, financial independence, or being a person of benevolence.

The famous story of Latorno, back when I was a kid, was an inspiring story. He finally got to the place where he could give away 90% of his income.

My mentor, Mr. Schoff, knew the story and said to me, "wouldn't that be great for you, Mr. Rohn? To finally get to the place where you could give away 90%?" I thought, 'wow that would be incredible.'

Somebody says, "90%. Wow that's a lot to give away." Well, you should have seen the 10% that was left. It was not peanuts.

But anyway, those kinds of dreams, those kinds of goals are what really start the fire.

At first you just need the goals that start triggering activity immediately.

Say, "I want to be able to pay my rent on time within 90 days. I'm putting in a little extra time. I'm doing this, I'm doing that. I'm taking the class. Whatever. After 90 days, I'm never going to be late on my rent again. I'm tired of the creditors calling. What are my goals?"

I heard a knock on my door back when I was about 24. I went to the door and there was a Girl Scout selling cookies. She gives me the big pitch. Girl Scouts, best organization in the world, we've got this variety of cookies, just $2.00. Then, with a big smile, she asked me to buy.

I wanted to buy. That wasn't a problem. Big problem, though, was I didn't have $2.00 in my pocket.

I was a grown man. I had a family. A couple of kids. I had been to college one year. I didn't have $2.00 in my pocket.

I didn't want to tell her I was that broke. So, I lied to her and said, "Hey, I've already bought lots of Girl Scout cookies. Still got plenty in the house."

So, she said, "Well, that's wonderful. Thank you very much," and she left.

When she left, I said to myself "I don't want to live like this anymore. How low can you get? Lying to a Girl Scout. I mean, that's about as low as you can go."

SO, that became an obsession for me.

From that day on I said, "I'm immediately going to acquire whatever it takes to have a pocket full of money so that no matter where I am for the rest of my life, no matter how many Girl Scouts are there, no matter how many cookies they've got to sell, I'll be able to buy them all."

It just triggered something.

Now, that's not a ranch in Montana. That's not becoming a billionaire. But, it was enough of an incentive to get me started.

Schoff taught me that you have to carry money in your pocket. He said, "$500 in your pocket feels better than $500 in the bank."

I couldn't wait 'til the moment when I had $500 in my pocket.

It doesn't take much to get started. Then the list goes on from there.

Then if you have enough of those reasons, don't tell me you won't get up early, stay up late, read the book, listen to the cassette, do the deal, take notes, keep a journal, work on your language, or work on your skills.

I'm telling you, it's all wrapped up there: dreams, visions, setting goals, starting with something simple.

When you talk about reasons, Jim, don't many of those strong reasons come out of a pain in one's life?

Sure.

Okay. Because I know from my own life that it can come from necessity and it can come out of pain and trying to get away from that.

The pain of not having $2.00 was pain enough.

Nobody else witnessed it, but me and the Girl Scout. Of course, I'm sure she didn't notice it because she accepted my lie and moved on.

But, I said, "I don't want this to happen anymore."

It was such an incredible resolve and it was only over $2.00. But it doesn't matter what it is. If it's something you want to correct, something you never want to happen again, that's the beginning.

You're well known internationally about the power of goals, the key formula for success.

Can you tell us about goals? The importance of goals, but more specifically, how do you set them? Do you think them? Do you write them down? Can you walk us through the power and the process of goal setting?

In my two-day leadership seminar, I go through a little workshop. It's called *Designing The Next Ten Years.*

It's really a simple process.

Start making lists of what you want.

I teach the simple, simple ways. Others have got some complicated ways of setting goals and deadlines and all that stuff. I don't do that.

I just say to make a list of the books you want to read. Make a list of the places you want to go. Start making a list of the things you wish to acquire.

What kind of education do you want for your family? Make a list.

Where are the place you want to visit? Make a list.

What kind of experiences do you want to have? Make a list.

Decide what you want. Then write it all down. Put a lot of little things on there so you can start checking some things off. Because part of the fun of having the list is checking it off. No matter how small it is.

My first list had a little revenge. Some of the people who said I couldn't do well. They went on my list. I couldn't wait to get my new car and drive it up on their lawn. A few little things on revenge.

It doesn't matter what it is. It's your personal list. You can tear it up and throw it away if you want and then get started on it.

Later you can say as you look back, "I was all hot on this idea. Now, here's something I know that is much better. I'm going to forget about that other thing." So, it's an ongoing, continual process.

But, I have discovered that if you think about the things you want" for you, your family, some goals are individual, some are collective, some are family, some are business, just start with that. Rearrange it any way you want to. You don't have to have any deadlines. You can look at the list after you've made it and start putting a 1, 3, 5 or 10 number beside each item. You know, "I think I can accomplish that in about a year. I think I can accomplish that in about three years. I think I can accomplish that in about five years." Something like that. But, it's easy.

Success is easy. Especially in America it's easy. Bangladesh, it's hard. Cambodia, it's hard. America, it's easy.

If you don't believe that, if you think easy is hard, then you are in trouble all your life.

We've got to teach our kids. Some of them have the concept that America is hard. They don't understand the difference between Bangladesh and America.

The average income in Bangladesh is about $100 a year. That's what's hard.

If you understand what's hard and what's easy, you can say, "Wow, it ought to be easy here."

The only reason for not doing well here, is not applying yourself for some information to learn, and then start to practice right away.

You've got to practice. You have to do the deal. You read this book on good health, right? It talks about nutrition and it talks about exercise Then in the middle of the book the author says, "Now reader, set this book aside. Fall on the floor and see how many push ups you can do." Then, of course, you don't do that. So, you read on and the author says, "If you didn't set this book aside and if you didn't fall

32

on the floor to see how many push ups you can do, why don't you just give this book away? Why bother yourself with reading if you're not going to pick an idea and try it?"
That's such great advice.

Ok, I want to bring something up and see if you agree with me on it.

We're talking about taking action. We're talking about planning, ambition, and taking those baby steps.

It seems to me, in my own personal life, when you start taking the steps, start changing your thinking, start moving forward toward a dream or vision, it almost seems like the universe conspires with you to help you. Do you see that as well?

Absolutely!
A phrase in the Bible seems to indicate that whatever you move towards, moves towards you.
It mentions that God said, 'if you make a move toward me, I'll make a move toward you.'
If you move toward education, it seems like the possibilities of education start moving your way.
If you move toward good health, the ideas for better health, the information starts moving toward you.
That's good advice.
If you'll just start the process of moving toward what you want, it is true, mysteriously, by some unique process, life loves to reward its benefactors.
If you start taking care of something, it wants to reward you by producing and looking well.
If you take care of flowers, they seem to bloom especially for you and say, "Look how pretty we are. You have taken such good care of us. Now we want to give back to you by giving you our beauty."
I taught my two girls how to swim and dive. Of course, like all kids, they'd say, "Daddy, watch me. Watch me do this dive." It's almost like they're saying, 'You're the one that taught me. You're the one that had patience with me. You invested part of your life in this process. Now watch me. Watch how good I am.'

33

All of life wishes to do that. All life wishes to *reward* its benefactor.

It could be something like a garden that grows because you took the time to cultivate it, to pull out the weeds, and take care of the bugs. Now, the garden does extremely well for you as a reflection back to you Because you are the one that invested time, energy, effort, and a piece of your life.

Let's stay here, Jim. Talk about the power of giving and the word "tithing". Can we talk about giving and what happens when someone gives?

I teach a little formula for kids called seventy, ten, ten, and ten.

This formula is about never spending more than 70 cents out of every dollar you earn.

The way it works is that ten cents is for active capital, ten cents is for passive capital, and then ten cents is to give away.

Whether it's to your church, a benevolent organization, or whether you let someone else manage it, or you manage it yourself.

We've got to teach generosity right from the beginning. I teach that ten percent is a good figure to start with.

You know when you become rich and wealthy, it can be 20, 30, 40, 50, 60, 70, 80, 90. Whatever.

But, ten cents is the start.

If you teach generosity, I'm telling you, kids will give you a dime out of every dollar to help someone that can't help themselves.

It's about what it does for you spiritually. Do it for what it brings back to you in terms of self-esteem.

Help to enrich the world by giving, and not only 10 percent of your money, but maybe some percentage of your time as well.

That investment is a smart investment.

It may bring returns to you immediately in ways you don't even know. It can do amazing things for your character, your reputation, and your inner spirit. It's all worth it!

34

Someone might say, "Well, I gave to this organization and they misused it."

It doesn't matter to you whether they misused it or not. The key for you is that you gave.

They've got to be responsible on there own side.

No matter what though, giving is a *major* piece. Then, the next step is giving somebody your ideas.

This mentor, I met when I was 25, Earl Schoff is someone I have to thank for the rest of my life for taking the time to share with me a bit of his philosophy that revolutionized my life.

I was never the same again after the first year. No one has ever had to say to me after the first year I was with him, 'when are you going to get going? When are you going to get off the dime?'

I've never heard that since that first year that I met this man who gave me his ideas and he did it freely.

He did it with great excitement. Because he knew that if he invested in me, I would probably invest in someone else.

Sure enough, that turned out to be true.

Ok. It's been 38 years or so. You're entering your second decade of doing this.

Where does the continuous passion and inspiration come from for you? Why are you still doing this?

It's very exciting because it's made me several fortunes and continues to do so.

But, part of the greatest excitement is when your name appears in somebody's testimonial.

You know, someone says something like, "I was at a certain place in my life and I listened to this person and it changed my life.

Mark Hughes, the founder of HerbalLife, used to say that because he attended my seminar when he was 19 it changed his life. He said, "I attended Jim Rohn's seminar and he was the first person that gave me the idea that in spite of my background I could make changes and become successful."

35

You can imagine how that made me feel. It's amazing for me to have my name appearing in his testimonial.

But, whether it's Mark Hughes or someone else, it doesn't matter.

Imagine this scenario: You've got someone who says, "let me introduce you to the person that changed my life five years ago. We were sitting at Denny's five years ago and he recommended this book to me. He told me that it has really helped him. SO, he recommended it to me. Well, as I look back on it now, that was the beginning of some incredible life changes for me. Look where I am today. I'm telling you, it started five years ago at Denny's on a Tuesday morning when this person introduced me to this book."

So, you don't have to give seminars. You don't have to give lectures. You don't even have to write books to affect someone's life and to do it so well that your name appears in their testimonial someday.

You know, someone says, "Here's the person who believed in me until I could believe in myself. Someone who saw more in me than I could see at the beginning."

Let's stay here, Jim. Because there's something I want to get across to people. It's such a powerful a statement that you talk about. I've heard you talk about the concept of sure, we want to reach our destination. We want to reach our goals. But, more importantly, Jim, can you talk about the power in the being and the becoming?

Well, true. What we acquire of course is valuable. But, the greatest value is not what we acquire. The greatest value is what we become.

My mentor had an interesting way of teaching it. When I was 25 years old he said, "I suggest, Mr. Rohn, that you set a goal to become a millionaire."

I was all intrigued by that. You know, it's got a nice ring to it - millionaire.

Then he said, "here's why…" I thought to myself, 'gosh, he doesn't need to teach me why. Wouldn't it be great to have a million dollars.' Then he said, "no then you'll never

36

acquire it. Here's why. Set a goal to become millionaire for what it makes of you to achieve it."

Can you say that again please?

"Set a goal to become millionaire for what it makes of you to achieve it."
He said, "Do it for the skills you have to learn and the person you have to become. Do it for what you'll end up knowing about the marketplace, what you'll learn about the management of time and working with people. Do it for the ability of discovering how to keep your ego in check. For what you have to learn about being benevolent. Being kind as well as being strong. What you have to learn about society and business and government and taxes and becoming an accomplished person to reach the status of millionaire.

All that you have learned and all that you've become to reach the status of millionaire is what's valuable. Not the million dollars.

If you do it that way, then once you become a millionaire, you can give all the money away. Because it's not the money that's really important. What's important is the person you have become."

That was one of the best pieces of philosophy I have ever heard in my life.

Nobody ever shared it with me like that before.

Another thing he said was, "beware of what you become in pursuit of what you want. Don't sell out. Don't sell out your principles. Don't compromise your values. Because you might acquire something by doing so, but it won't taste good."

An old prophet said, "sometimes what tastes good in the mouth finally turns bitter in the belly." Then, later we regret that we compromised or that we did something incredibly wrong to acquire something. It's not worth it. If we do that, then what we get is worthless.

If you use something like that to challenge yourself to grow, to reach a certain level, I think it's wise. Because then

37

you know where the true value is and that is in the person you become.

I want to reverse back to about 90 seconds ago when you were talking about your great mentor, Earl Nightingale. You talked about the ability to express gratitude. To express thanks.

I feel, in my own life, an aspect of gratitude is very important.

So, number one, do you agree with that, and two, can you talk about the power of that word - gratitude?

Well, it absolutely is very important.

I made a little list the other day as I reminisced about the things that really made such an incredible contribution to my life.

Number one on my list, of course, was my parents.

I was an only child. They spoiled me. They laid a foundation for me that has kept me steady all these years.

The more I thought about it, I thought, 'what a contribution they've made to my life.'

A lot of it, at the moment, I couldn't see. I didn't realize. But, as the years began to unfold, I realized that what they taught me, the care they gave me, the love they shared with me, that no matter what happened to me, I always had a place I could always go home to.

They provided that kind of unique stability.

They didn't just say, 'son, you can do it.' It was also the advice they gave me and the prayers they sent me, no matter where I went around the world, cause I believe in that, the power of prayer.

Every once in awhile I get a letter and someone says, "Mr. Rohn, we are praying for you." I read it and think, 'Wow. This is some kind of letter when someone takes the time to say a prayer."

My gratitude for that is just unending.

Talk about the power of prayer.

Who knows, you know, the mystery of prayer and God.

38

In the Declaration of Independence it says, we are created equal. But it says also that, we are endowed by our creator with gifts and rights.

It's a philosophy America believes in that we are a special creation. That we have these gifts based on a creator.

We open the Senate with prayer. We put on our money "In God We Trust." We are that kind a nation really.

When I travel the world, people ask me, "how come America does so well?" I say, "read the money." I think that is probably part of it. That kind of trust, that kind of In God We Trust, implies prayer and I think that it is so vital.

It doesn't have to be in a church, synagogue, mosque, or anywhere else. It doesn't have to be in a formal place. But, I think it's a tremendous power.

We're talking about the power of thankfulness, of gratitude.

Jim, I want to put on my world famous, internationally-renowned, two-minute warning with you. All that means is we have about ten minutes left to rock n roll, and shake and bake.

Let's talk about the best kept secret of the rich, time management. Tell me about the importance of it and how we become effective time managers.

Well, first is to realize how precious time is.

There's not an unending supply of years in your life.

My father lived to be 93 and it still seemed very short. I kept asking for another ten years, another ten years, another five years.

Surely, Papa can live to be 100 I'd think.

I'd love to have him see the 21st Century, which was not to be. But, ninety-three years still seems short.

The Beatles wrote, "life is very short." For John Lennon it was extra short.

There is not an unending supply of the days and the moments.

The key is to utilize them to the best of your ability. Don't just to let them slip away. Capture them, like we capture the seasons. There is only so many.

39

In ninety years you have ninety spring times. If some guy says, you know, "I got twenty more years." You say, "no. You got twenty more times."

If you go fishing once a year you only have twenty more times to go fishing. Now that starts to make it a bit more critical. Not that I have a whole twenty more years, but just twenty more times. How valuable do I want to make these twenty times?

It doesn't matter whether it's going to the concert or sitting down with your family, or taking a vacation. There is only so many.

It's easy not to plan and do the details necessary to make them the best possible.

Then I have other little ideas like, 'don't start the day, until you have it finished.'

Say that again, Jim.

Don't start the day until you have it finished.
It's a key for executives, a key for leadership. But it's also a key for a mother at home. It doesn't matter, whoever.

Plan the day to the best of your abilities.

There will be plenty of room for surprises and innovations and whatever.

Give a good plan, a good schedule for the day.

Because each day is a piece of the mosaic of your life.

You can either just cross your fingers and say, "I hope it will work out okay," or you can give it some attention and say, "here's what I would like to accomplish in the next twenty four hours."

Just look at it that way and do a lot of it up front or maybe the night before. Start the day after you finished it.

It's like building a house. If I asked you, "when should you start building the house that you want to build?" and you say to me, "well, that's a good question. When should I start building the house?" I've got an excellent answer for you. The answer is, you start building it as soon as you have it finished.

40

You know, someone might say, "is it possible to finish a house before you start it?" The answer is, yes. It would be foolish to start it until you had it finished.

Imagine if you just started laying bricks. Somebody could come by and ask, "what are you building here?" You say, "I have no idea. I'm just laying bricks and well see how it works out." They would call you foolish and maybe take you away to a safe place.

The key is that it's possible to finish a day before you start it. It's possible to finish a month before you start it.

I do business around the world with colleagues in about 50 countries. To do business around the world in 50 countries you can't imagine all of the preparatory planning that has to be done. Some things are three years, five years, two years, one year ahead in order to do that kind of global business.

But, if you just learned to be disciplined enough to start with the day plan, the month plan, your good health plan, I'm telling you, you will take advantage of time like you can't believe.

Jim, let's bring up a few topics and go 30 to 45 seconds on each, if we can.

You're one of the most effective communicators of the last 50 years or so. You've talked in front of 4 million people and you've influenced millions beyond that through your books and tapes.

What's the most important communication tip you can give us right now?

You just need a desire to be a great communicator and keep improving the art every day.

It's easy to be careless with your language in social areas, but that's going to affect your business.

You just have to start practicing the art of better language, whether it's social, personal, home, or family.

You can't say, "oh, it's with my family, so my language doesn't really matter." It really does matter because it's so valuable for them. But, also because it's so valuable for you to practice the art.

It's like this telephone conversation. If I thought, 'well, I don't have 35,000 people to talk to. So, I'll treat this conversation carelessly.' I just learn not to do that.

I want to give the most concise and best information I can, even though it's a telephone conversation and not a big audience in some auditorium.

So, we're talking here about being on purpose, about changing language, changing your mindset. When a person goes for something, there are roadblocks to steer away from. There are adversities. Talk about the power of resilience.

You've just got to be able to come back. Come back from a disappointment. It takes a bit of courage.

If you start a sales career and the first person you approach says, "no", you've got to have the courage to talk to the second person.

If you start a little business, set up the first meeting, and nobody joins, you've got to have the courage to say, "I'll set up another meeting. Because if one person says no it doesn't mean everybody's going to say no."

You've just got to have that ability to come back.

You've got to understand the law of averages. Not everybody is going to be interested in your project. Not everybody is going to buy your product.

You can't take it personally.

Then, if you get hit by poor health, you've just got to do everything within your power to get well.

If you face a disappointment, you've got to come back. From a divorce, you've got to come back. It's going to hurt for awhile, you've got to let it linger and do whatever it's going to do. But, then you've got to build back.

That's part of the game of life.

It's no different for you, me, or anyone else.

Resilience, we all need it. Whether it's health, marriage, family, business, social, or personal.

Talk about the power of enlightened self-interest.

42

Yes, life doesn't give us what we need. Life gives us what we deserve.

If you want wealth, it's okay to wish for wealth *if* you pay the proper price for wealth.

So, there is a price to be paid.

You can pay the proper price without diminishing anyone else. Once I learned that, I got excited about being wealthy in my own self-interest. Everybody wins.

What we're talking about here is coming from a position of integrity and creating wealth for the benefit of others.

I ask this question to a lot of the people, Mark Victor Hansen, Robert Allen, and a lot of the people I have interviewed. I always thought it was a melancholy question, but they have told me it isn't. We're all going to pass on some day. What do you want the world to say about Jim Rohn when that day does come?

That he invested his life wisely and as best he could to help as many people to change their lives as possible and that he blessed his own life. That's really it.

You talk about self-education. You talk about how it's the seed of fortune. Are there any books out there, in addition to your own at jimrohn.com, that you can recommend to my audience?

Well, sure. Schoff recommended *Think and Grow Rich* to me when I first started learning.

What was the most powerful thing you took out of *Think and Grow Rich*?

Desire, determination, preset plans, never give up, persistence, it's got a wealth of information in it.

Anything else come to mind?

The Richest Man in Babylon helped me to become a millionaire by age 32. Simple little book. Easy to follow. Inspiring. *The Richest Man in* Babylon, by George Clauson.

Jim, we're wrapping down the show tonight. Jim, it's been an absolute goldmine and a pleasure to share you with my audience. Jim Rohn, thank you very much for appearing on The Mike Litman Show.

It's been a pleasure, Mike. We'll do it again sometime.

46

Chapter Two

Conversation with
Mark Victor Hansen

(Introduction to listeners...)

I gotta tell you that in a moment I'm going to bring on one of the most magnetic, charismatic and just awesome individuals. I gotta tell you this, we have some of the top people on our show every week. But the individual I'm going to bring on in a moment is just absolutely dynamic. This individual you know from his best-selling book *Chicken Soup for the Soul*. He's sold millions and millions of copies. Now it's almost Chicken Soup for everything. Chicken Soup for the Pets, the Women, the Men. It's just absolutely awesome. But hear this, the goal of this interview is to give you some other information on this individual that you don't know. This individual is also the author of, *Dare to Win*. He has an unbelievable audio-cassette series called, *Unlimited Riches*. *Visualizing is Realizing*, is another one of his incredible audio cassette series. One of my favorite books he's written is called, *How to Achieve Total Prosperity*. Another great book he did is called, *The Miracle of Tithing*. He just totally has been a huge impact in my life. I'd like to welcome, Mark Victor Hansen.

(To Mark)

Welcome, Mark.

After listening to you, I want to hear me.

It's funny Mark, I mean, I'm totally excited and just really happy that you are on the phone right now.

I'm honored Mike. I'm thankful. It was my dream and prayer that some day I'd get to talk to people who cared about things that matter.

Thank you, Mark. I have to start out by telling you that I truly believe you are the Michael Jordan of the self-improvement industry.

I wish you would put that in writing and send it to me. By the way, Michael Jordan is also my hero.

He's incredible.

Exactly.

Awesome! I just dug his persistence.

I've been through a lot of your stuff. You've impacted my life very transformationally.

I want to hear a very different Mark on this show.

Chicken Soup for the Soul has absolutely just taken over America. You can't walk into a bookstore without piles and piles and piles of books. And you do a lot of interviews. I'm sure a lot of radio and TV. Everyone's talking about *Chicken Soup for the Soul*.

What I want to do is, I want to start a couple of years back and make our way there.

Okay. You lead, I'll follow.

Sounds like a great plan.

You wrote something 17 years ago, Mark, that is my favorite book you've ever written. It's just eye opening to me. I've probably referred 10 people to call your 800 number to get the book, *How to Achieve Total Prosperity*. It sold hundreds of thousands of copies, and it's just such an impactful book.

Let me ask you this question, Mark. At that point in your life, before we get into the book, at that point in your life, why did you write the book? And what does it mean to you today?

48

It means everything to me.

Because, first of all, I think everybody deserves prosperity. Just this week I learned the first line in the Upanishads. Which is the, I happen to be Christian, but the first line in the Upanishads, which is the Hindi Bible equivalent, says, "Out of abundance he took abundance and still abundance remains."

What I am saying is that there is prosperity enough for everybody. It's not how big a piece of the pie you can get, Calvert Roberts taught me, it's how big you make the pie.

Once I caught onto prosperity, I had to write about it because I said "Holy cow, this isn't available to me."

Once you are out of lack and limitation and shortage, you bust out of that, you start to say, "Hey, wait a second, there's enough for everybody."

I mean Ted Turner is getting richer, and has only helped me get richer.

Michael Jordan getting richer has helped every athlete get richer, because they are charging more and having agencies.

A guy like Bill Gates, last year in his company he made twenty-one thousand millionaires INSIDE Microsoft! Is that incredible?

Let's talk about Bill Gates, since you bring him up.

I'm a fan.

Yeah, I've seen all your videos and all that. Talk about how imagination has totally transformed Microsoft. Can you tell us about that?

Well, Bill Gates. Here's a little nerdy kid who starts out. He's 16 years old. He's very bright and at Harvard.

I teach that you gotta have a team and have a dream, and a little bit of a scheme, and then you'll go out and realize it. And that's exactly what he did.

He and Paul Allen got together.

49

And he now says, "the only asset of Microsoft", which also means your only asset, my only asset, and every listener's only asset, "is human imagination."

Human imagination created all the books that I have done. Whether it's Chicken Soup. Or all the software that Bill Gates does. It creates the cable stuff that Ted Turner does.

Now, Ted Turner owns 1% of America and the first line in his book says, "Every year I work until I earn a billion dollars. It takes 15 days, and I'm done for the year."

Now, that's a level of use of imagination beyond where I am today. But I'll subscribe to it and I believe based on what I'm pulling off today, that I'll get there.

But I wouldn't have gotten there if I hadn't read that line from Ted Turner.

Let's stay with the concept of the prosperity. It's something not taught in schools and something you almost have to search for, to find out what it truly is.

Prosperity is a Latin word, it means 'to be in the flow.' And everyone of us is in the flow when we are thinking right, talking right, acting right, and living right. We get the right results, right here, and right now.

And when you think negatively, you're into immobilization.

When you're thinking positively and correctly, you're into mobilization and you start taking right action to get right results!

Absolutely awesome!

I want to touch on Prosperity Principle #10 in your book, *How to Achieve Total Prosperity*. Because, you say when you learned this information you HAD to put it into a book.

When I learn things from you, I'm calling up my friends across the country, and I'm like, "You gotta read this or hear this!"

Number 10 is: 'Teach what you most want to learn and need to learn.' Could you expand on the power of that principal?

One of the things that was flashing in my head is that, I've been a professional speaker now for 25 years, and my wife and I were down in the oil country, Midland Odessa, Texas back during the boom. The poorest guy in the room is worth over $10 million and I had just become a millionaire.

Everyone of them was given one of my books, one of the guys liked me talking.

What happened is, they all had money, but they didn't have prosperity feeling, which is what I teach.

See, if you have ful-<u>feel</u>ment and ful-<u>thrill</u>ment, you get <u>fulfilment</u> is the way I teach it.

And what's incredible here is, these old boys were listening in rapt attention, but right before I started talking to them about how to achieve total prosperity, my wife leaned over and said, "Are you sure you're the right guy to talk to them?"

So all of us get tested, and what's interesting is: teach what you most need to learn and you'll do it. That is what I teach at every seminar I do, whether it's a sales seminar or management seminar or leadership seminar.

I say, "gain at least one idea, just one. You don't have to like me. Just get an idea out of here that you like and then go do something with it and then teach it to one other person and you'll take ownership of it."

Whenever you teach what you learn, it becomes more of you.

Exactly.

It becomes more of you. You walk and talk it. It's amazing. That's dynamite stuff!

What I like to do, is add some information that's not so easily found; that's really the heart and soul of what my guests do.

Something I think is so powerful and normal in America today, you talk about it, it's what you describe as money scripts, negative money scripts. Like, 'What do you think, I'm Rockefeller?', or a penny saved is a penny earned.'

51

I just think most people aren't aware. Their self-awareness isn't high enough that they realize when these things are said.

Take a moment and just talk to my audience.

What are money scripts and how are we programmed at an early age about that?

> Well, my parents were immigrants from Denmark, and while I love them totally and absolutely, my dad said all the stuff you said. "We can't afford that or that or that." "Who do you think I am, Rockefeller? You think I'm made of money?" "What do you think, money grows on trees?" Which is actually where the money we use, paper money, comes from. "You can nickel and dime me to death," and the key one is "You better save your money for a rainy day."
>
> These are all examples of negative programming that doesn't benefit anyone.
>
> I teach indifference to all that. I'm not making fun of the people, but all of us have got to laugh at our situations cause we are all in the same human situation.
>
> Our foibles are funny if you take the right glance at them.

I agree.

Now, Mark, you wrote a book, it's a small book. I got it through your office.

I just feel like it's impactful, it's powerful if you use the principles. Getty, and a lot of the great barons and fortunes of yesteryear used this principle.

The book is called, *The Miracle of Tithing*.

Can you talk about the power of 'tithing'? Should you give WITH expectations? WITHOUT expectations? Can you talk a little bit about that? The concept of tithing, where it comes from and how people can use it in their own lives?

> Absolutely!
>
> First of all, tithing is an ancient concept. It goes through absolutely every religion and spiritual system.
>
> It says, God gives you 100%, you are supposed to take 10% and give it back to God.

52

When you do that, "you take a little step towards God," as my friend Jim Rohn says, "and God takes a God step toward you."

It doesn't matter if you do it with expectations or without expectations.

It's just like all the research right now on whether or not praying helps. One of my friends, Dr. Larry Dawsey, deals with people with cancer and he says, "it doesn't matter what religion you are. It doesn't matter whether the people know you are praying for them or not. Prayer just makes people well." He's done all these double-blind studies.

Well, the minute you tithe, you open up all the universe to you, because it changes your attitude; but also because every cause has an effect. And it's got a third part to it: A total result that you can't even start to know. The beautiful thing about the total result is that it compounds.

It's like your investing and you're getting an equity with God and good and universe. What happens is the minute you do that, you know you are going to win!

Mark, can you tithe only money?

No, as a matter of fact, good question, great question, Michael.

The truth is, you can tithe money, time, energy, effort. Whatever your need more of is what you need to tithe some.

I started, on Long Island, when I built this business.

So, I was bankrupt and upside down and I got with a 26-year-old speaker who is still doing a brilliant job out there, Chip Collins.

Let me give you his story, with his permission. I'm sure he'd let me tell you this.

When he was first starting his speaking business out on Long Island, he's got a wife and two little babies. He's got absolutely no money, and he didn't know what to do.

He's got 35 cents in his pocket, and he's Catholic, so he goes in the Catholic church and he goes, "35 cents, I can't even buy milk for my little babies and feed my wife. I don't know what I'm going to do." And he's crying and he's sitting in the front pew and he goes, "Okay, God, I'm going to give you all 35 cents. I haven't got anything else. You get all the last pennies to my name and if you can make this work for me, I'll do whatever you say. I don't know what to do."

He gives the 35 cents, then he's walking out of the church and a guy in the last pew said, "Chip, Chip, come here!" Chip says, "Do you know me?"

And he says, "Yeah, you came in and asked if you could do a talk in my office last week." Jim says, "Oh yeah, right, right, right."

And he says, "I've decided I want to hire you for eight talks because business has been really good lately. Do you mind if I give you a check and pre-pay you right now?"

And he got a check for $400, which was like $4 million, because he went out and bought milk for his babies, and food for his wife, and could pay the bills that month. It was that immediate.

When he rolled up there, he had tears in his eyes, and he's pounding the steering wheel, going, "I'm a failure. I'm destroyed. I'm no good. I'm nothing and I'm lower than dirt."

Wow! That's an absolute example of the power of tithing! It's fair to say, Mark, that you use tithing a lot in your own life?

Totally! Even as an example, we won't do any books that we don't pre-agree on what our charity of choice is going to be on the book.

Okay, let's go to an area that I believe is a passionate area that you like to speak about.

I've learned about this individual just from hearing you speak about him so much.

One of your biggest mentors was the great Buckminster Fuller. I know you speak about him and he was very impactful in your life.

Can you tell our listeners how he impacted your life, and what one or two things that you take away from your relationship with him that will just live with you forever?

Totally.

Bucky Fuller was the Leonardo da Vinci of our time. He was Albert Einstein's best student. He had 2,000 major inventions, like geodesic domes, that everyone has seen. They're the buildings made out of triangles. He had rolling needles. Dimaxium cars that would go, I'm giving this to you off the top of my head, but I think 187 miles per gallon on alcohol methanol.

In other words, we got to get off the petrochemical expedient. And I know all the petrochemical companies that are listening now are going, "What, what, what?!" But, the truth is, we have got to grow our stuff and get to income energy.

I was at Southern Illinois University in Graduate School. I was doing some inventions, going through the SIU Foundation and a guy said, "Dr. Fuller is on the faculty here.

He's an inventor and you're an inventor, why don't you come hear him speak?" I went and heard this guy who is diminutive in height. He was already mature - he was 71 at the time. He had a closely cropped head, but he just had a whole glow.

He had 5,000 students and I was sitting in the front with Dr. Richard, who took me there. And I was just in awe.

Within two weeks, I was a research staff member of Dr. Fuller. I traveled around the world with him for the next seven years. He helped me learn how to think comprehensively.

He had created a concept called, World Game. How do you make the world work for 100% of humanity? And I'm still trying to out picture that. And that is why every one of our books has a different charity tied to it, whether we want to feed unfed humanity, or house unhoused humanity.

With 'Chicken Three' we worked with the American Red Cross. I was a spokesperson and an idea guy for them for awhile. And we raised a 1/4 million dollars just in the first year for them.

We got all my chiropractic friends, which is very big in the chiropractic market place in Long Island. We just got almost every doctor to do a blood drive and give a free adjustment if they had a blood mobile at their place and we raised enough blood.

They were out of blood and we got their blood back. Is that cool?

That's really cool.

All it takes is exactly where we were a minute ago is: *imagination creates reality*. If you will not get stuck in the problem and you start saying how? What would be ten outrageous, crazy, outlandish solutions? Then write them all down and stay in theory, just for a minute, and then use your best thinking to prioritize it.

Because Bucky always said, "every priority has an anti-priority". Meaning that, if you're doing something you can't be doing something else at the same time. Like, I can't be talking to you and also be babysitting or something.

Well let's stay on that for a second, you mention imagination and you have a simple four step success plan. Can you talk about that?

Sure. Four principles: First of all, you've got to figure out what you really want. In my case and in Jack's case, we didn't want a best-selling book. We wanted a mega best-selling book, *Chicken Soup for the Soul*. Beyond that, we didn't really want a best-selling book, we wanted to make a best-selling *series*. The clearer you are, the easier it is to execute. So number one, you figure out what you really want. Number two, you put it in writing and where I differ from all of my peers is, I say you got to have too many goals. I've got over 6,000 goals in writing.

6,000 goals!?

Most people say, "all I want is a new car." When you were 16, Michael, you said, "Well, if I get a car the girls will like me." And then you get a car and you find out that they want something else. [Laughs]

56

So, figure out what you want. Number two, put it in writing. Three, visualize it. Flip Wilson said, "What you see is what you get." We're talking about what you see with your inner eye. We cut out the New York Times Bestseller list. Then we put our names at the top before we ever got to the top in real life. Then we put it on my mirror and we put one up at Jack's office, on his mirror. So in our mind's eye, when we were shaving, or the ladies were doing cosmetics, we owned the concept that we were best-selling authors before we actually were best-selling.

Stay there for a second. The concept of 'being' before you have it. And what you're ready for is ready for you. Can you just walk us through that?

Absolutely!
I have pictures of Walt Disney on my wall here in my office.
During the last days of Walt Disney's life, right before he died, a guy came in to see him. The guy comes in and says, "Oh Walt, it's so terrible, you're not going to get to see Epcot and Disney World." And Walt looks at him and says, "Are you kidding me? If I didn't see it my mind, you'll never see it in your experience."
This telephone call that you and I are having now was your vision before it happened. And it was my vision at two levels. My vision was that I get to do publicity, talk to people that care, that really want to make a difference in their life. Your vision was to have people who could really do celebrated thinking so that people out there listening could get an exalted idea, continue listening and your show gets to keep growing, so it's a win, win, win. All three of us are winning.

Absolutely. Well, let's touch on the brother of visualization, which is affirmation. Now, number one, do you use affirmations in your own life? And number two, what's the proper way to move forward on that?

Affirmations have always got to be in the first person, singular. They've got to be "I AM", because they're the strongest words in the world.

If you are poor, you've got to start affirming quietly and privately to yourself, "I'm rich." If you're sick, you've got to say, "I'm healthy." And you've got to visualize that the doctor is going to come in and say, "congratulations, you've overcome that dreaded disease", or whatever the problem is.

Or visualize who's going to give you the trophy or award and say, "Boy, you've got the number one business show on the air." Somebody will say that to you in the future. Who is that person?

That's what you've got to visualize and be quietly and inwardly affirming, because the spiritual line is that signs follow, they don't preceed. What happens is, they follow. And the other great spiritual line is: "your words shall not return to you void. But you go out and accomplish the mission whereon to you send it." What it means is that most people think, 'well, I can talk and it doesn't matter. When I talk right now, it goes into history.' It's just the opposite, it goes into the future!

So, what we're saying right now is that, we're going to sell a million books in one day. We are going to sell a million books, raise a million bucks for charity and feed a million kids all in one day in America. We got a new book: *Chicken Soup for the Kid's Soul.*

By the way, I expect you to come to one of the signings and sign books on our behalf.

I'm there already.

Isn't that cool?

Fantastic.

Mark, there's something about you as a person that fascinates me.

It seems to me that you just develop instant rapport with people.

58

How do you go about developing that type of rapport with people?

Well, that goes along with the four principles that we're covering:

Figure out what you want, write it down, and visualize it.

Then, the fourth one, you take your two index fingers, and one and one equals the power of 11. When you've got your team together, you get your dream together. And two people can create miracles.

Jack and I, and the team that I've created, all visualize that I'm not there for me, I'm there for the audience. In this case, I'm here for your audience.

What I'm saying is, that we need to have instant rapport, so we can have a fast start and really go somewhere.

Usually, in the professional speeches I've got, even the stuff on videotapes, it's usually limited to an hour.

What I learned from Bucky Fuller is that, we call that, 'a good start!' [laughs]

It's like right now, you've got people out there listening to us going, "Oh man, I've got to have more of this stuff! This is really good!" So, they'll go up on your website and my website and they'll call our offices and they'll start. And what they are going to find out is that I've got 55 hours of non-duplicated information.

They'll go, 'nobody can know 55 hours worth of stuff.' But, every day I've decided that, not only am I going to write for two hours, not only am I going to write a quote everyday, but I'm going to create at least one new model that I can talk about for an hour.

So, I grow just one idea at a time and keep expanding it and exploring it.

My staff and I were just down in the conference room right before I got on the call with you and we've just shown the new slides that we've created today, which is called the Tetrahedron of Success, which says, 'what do you want? Write it down, visualize it, dream it, team it and scheme it, and it's yours.'

59

This is just absolutely awesome.

(To listeners)

For those of you listening, hearing about these books and saying, "how do I get my hands on them? How do I instantly wrap my hands around these awesome pearls of knowledge and life changing information?" What you want to do now is, you need to write this number down. This is Mark Victor Hansen's office...1-800-433-2314.

(Back to Mark)

Mark, you talk about team work a lot, the power of mastermind. You talk about how one and one doesn't equal two, it equals 11, and goes up exponentially from there. Two things: talk a little bit about masterminding. How does somebody go about finding the perfect masterminding partner?

It starts back with you. And the self-discovery is this: You've got to figure out who you are. You've got to figure out what is your greatest talent? What is your greatest unique ability?

My unique ability is that I'm unusual and unique as a speaker and a writer, promoter, and marketer. Those are the four things I can do.

I can't play golf. There is more I can't do than I can do.

Then you've got to find out the second part, it's the part that no one wants to explore in their journal. I wrote a whole book about doing it. It's a journal called, 'Future Diary'. You have to explore and ask yourself, 'where am I weak?" Nobody wants to admit where they are weak, but you've got to write down where you are weak.

Then you say, "I'm going to find somebody that's unique where I'm weak." Now one and one equals 11.

In the Mark and Jack team, where we write *Chicken Soup* and *Dare to Win* and books like that together, I'm basically the outside guy.

Jack can do that too, so I don't want to misstate it, but he's basically the inside guy. I'm a macro thinker. He's a micro thinker. I'm the imagination. He's the realization and implementation.

That doesn't make one better than the other. We are together and that's more important. We are a team, and we are a 50/50 team. Everything we do is shared.

It's not an issue, if he goes on Barbara Walters show and everyone says, "Well don't you feel bad?" Well, look I got to be on Mike's show, I got to be on...

The famous Mike Litman Show.

Exactly. He didn't get to go on this show, I did.

And the people listening and the host cares about you more than any other show. Let's talk about this; I heard you talk about it in a video of yours, which is available by calling 1-800-433-2314, which obviously is the gateway to financial freedom.

Mark, you talk a lot about Napoleon Hill, the great author of *Think and Grow Rich*. I heard you talking and you've read a lot of his essays with Edison and Ford, is that right?

I read all the original stuff. I read Think and Grow Rich probably 200 times. Chip Collins, who I talked about, is my mastermind partner there in Long Island. We talked about it endlessly. And the mind blower is, remember I said, "cause affects total result?" The mind blower is, the last couple of Napoleon Hill annual awards meetings, I've been the MC in a black tie along with my friend Wally 'Famous' Amos, who is the godfather of chocolate chip cookies.

He wrote a book called, *My Face Launched a Thousand Chips*.

I think he also wrote a book called, *The Man With No Name*.

That's right. Because he sold his name by accident. So, he started the *No Name Cookie Company*, which in Hawaii-an means Noname'. So, he has the *No Name Cookie Company* now.

61

What are the exceptional characteristics that you saw flowing through the individuals that Napoleon Hill interviewed?

> Everyone of them had *a sense of desperation toward a destination*. That's what I've got. I'm desperate to help people and my destination is to help people.

When you talk on stage and you're in front of an audience, there is such an element of interaction in that lecture room. It's absolutely amazing.

I want to talk to Mark Victor Hanson, the speaker, right now.

You use a technique, I believe it's called, 'call backs'. You have people touching themselves and saying things.

Tell a little about the power of call backs and how that works and how to go about doing that.

> Wonderful!
>
> I was going to ask you what you saw in me that caused rapport. What I ask people to do is, I ask them to touch themselves. That is called an *anchor*. And it wakes them up to a different level.
>
> Because I want people to repeat, "I'm healthy, I'm happy, I'm successful." What we learned from my friend Deepak Chopra, who is probably the greatest medical doctor, quantum physicist, and ayurvedic healer.
>
> Deepak says, (faking Indian accent) "happy thinking causes happy cells, happy cells, happy quanta, happy quanta causes everything else to be happy." [Laughing]
>
> I do his accent okay I think. I studied in India for a year, so I got the Indian accent down.
>
> I'm certainly not making fun. I'm just saying that everyone of us needs to decide whether you are going to be happy or sad, whether you are going to be successful or a failure.
>
> You've got to say, "goodbye to poverty, hello to riches." You've got to say, "goodbye to sickness, hello to health. Goodbye to limitedness and hello to unlimitedness."

62

There are plenty of examples around at every level. Whether its spiritual, mental, physical, financial. All of it exists and there is total prosperity available to each of us individually. Then when we all find it individually, we have it collectively.

Can you talk about money as energy?

That's all money is, is energy.

The simplest form that I see is called, 'the velocity of money.'

If we had a seminar and there's 400 people in front of me right now. I take the front row and I take out a dollar. One dollar bill and I buy something from you, Michael, and I had you buy something from Sam, and Sam buys from Sally, it goes on everybody's financial statement.

But Harry gets the dollar and goes, "Oh, my God. I read the New York Times. I don't believe it. We are going to go into a recession tomorrow. We've had a boom market too long, there's got to be a downside."

What happens is that, Harry here locks up that one dollar, stops it, and it doesn't go in the other 395 people's financial statements. Whereas what I'm teaching is just the opposite.

I teach the answer to the question, based on affirmations. Like you're saying, "How's business?" The answer is, "Booming." Because it's always booming for someone, somewhere, somehow, somenow.

Right now, America is in the greatest boom in history. It depends on what city you live in, but basically America's unemployment is 4.4%, down to 3%, down to 2% in some places and we are importing foreigners just to work.

Because what happens, is that we are the thinking capital of the world. The whole imagination thing that Bill Gates talked about. We were talking about it earlier.

There is no limit to imagination. As long as people imagine positively, we get more software, more books, more tapes, more videos, more games, more recreation. New ideas. And it's exciting. We'll go do great stuff.

Awesome. I wish this interview was four hours.

I want to stay right here. You as a professional speaker, a lot of times I do this show because there are questions and things I want to know. I love sharing the information with my audience.

You, the professional speaker, Mark, what do you think is the most persuasive technique that you know, that you use in your communication?

Stories. That's exactly why we did the whole Chicken Soup series.

Jason Oman, had a question to ask you, Mark.

Ask. Please.

It's an interesting question. He asks, "Mark, what do you look forward to in the morning when you wake up? What are the first thoughts out of your mind in the mornings?"

Well, I believe that everybody ought to get up just a little bit earlier than they usually would get up. Maybe go to the restroom. Then come back and meditate, cogitate, ruminate, and pray about your day for 15 minutes to a half hour. Do it before you really start your day. And do it in quietude. A quiet environment where you're not distracted.

You should make sure that your day is going to be the ideal day for you. Imagine in your mind, you come backwards through the day.

So you figure out when you are going to be going to bed later that day. You come through and you see every event working equal to or better than you even expect.

Like this interview is way better than I could have even dreamt of.

I hope you will interview me a lot in the future, because you've got such good energy and such a positive buzz. And you're so scholarly. Anybody you interview has got to be flattered and honored that you know their stuff so well.

By the way, as you know, I've done over 2,500 interviews since the Chicken Soup series has been up and running and I've got to tell you, I can tell the interviewers who care. Because they read your stuff.

I couldn't agree with you more and that's one of the things I take pride in here.

You do your homework.

Thanks, Mark. Ok, we have 10 minutes left. This is my two minute warning. I know you love to tell stories, but I'm going to ask for short answers as concise as possible.

Please. Go ahead.

You do a lot of sales training. It's one of your things that you do.

I love selling. Since I was nine years old. That's 41 years I've been selling now.

What one or two little bullets or points of wisdom can you give my listeners right now about selling?

Selling has just a couple aspects to it. You've got to prospect, present, persuade and close.
When you've got a name, you've got a suspect. Everybody has got to have a big list of who they're going to call on. It's the same whether if you are trying to get a loan or whatever. If you are trying to borrow money, you know, always test yourself out on a bank that you don't want to get the loan from.
Go to some of the lesser banks. What you will be amazed at is they might be nicer to you than the bigger banks.
Okay, so you've got a suspect.
When you are with somebody by telephone or live, you've got a prospect.

When they buy, they become a customer.

When they re-buy, recommend and refer you, you've got a client.

What you want is a client who becomes life-long. You want a life-long client, friend.

I don't want somebody to buy just one Chicken Soup or one Aladdin book. I want them hopefully to read my whole series.

I can tell you a hundred authors that I'm addicted to. We already mentioned Napoleon Hill. I've read everything he's written. I've read all the tracks and the ancillary stuff.

Because if you really get into it, you want to follow a person like you've followed me, and see how much do they know.

I know you're not just following me, you've got hundreds of people with information that you put into your head.

The more input that you get, the better output you can have and the more choices you can make. Because I've read over 50,000 books and the guy who turned me on to reading, my teacher from my high school, was just here. I took him on a tour.

The guy wept because he thought, "Hey, it worked."

Now 30 years later he's seen the output of his teaching.

I'm afraid the trouble with teaching is that you can't see what's going to happen with your students until you're already retired. Most of the time anyway.

Let me ask you this. *Think and Grow Rich*. If you can take one nugget out of that book, one tactic, technique, or mental strategy, what would it be?

Napoleon Hill, on his dying bed, said two things. Number one, "you gotta have a definite major purpose." That means a goal bigger than you. One that lets you score at a level that is going to make a difference and leave a legacy.

And number two is, "you gotta have a team together." He called it, "a master-mind alliance." In Japan they call it, "quality circles." It doesn't matter what you call it, it matters that you do it.

66

Now, it's funny, we're 43 minutes into this interview. And, we haven't talked about the mega bestsellers, *Chicken Soup for the Soul*. Fantastic book! Everyone has a copy out there. If they don't, they need to go grab one. How did the title come about, Mark?

> We learned from Napoleon Hill. He had a title on his book called, 'How to Make a Boodle with Your Noodle.' The publisher in Philadelphia hated the idea.
> So, Napoleon Hill had like 228 titles. None of them worked.
> He meditated and programmed his subconscious. He said to himself 400 times, "Best-selling title. Best-selling title."
> So we did the same thing. Except we said, "Mega best-selling title" 400 times.
> Four o'clock in the morning, Jack comes up with it. Gets goose bumps. He tells his wife, Dr. Georgia. Calls me at 4:30 and said, "I think I got it."
> I got goose bumps and couldn't go back to sleep, the title was so good.
> Then 33 publishers in New York said, "Get outta here. Nobody buys short stories."

And then Health Communications took you guys, right?

> Well, we sold it ourselves, because our agent fired us in New York. And we love him, he's a great man. But, he said, "the book is never going to sell. 33 rejections. I've spent enough time with you guys. Get out of here." So, it's fine. We sold it ourselves.

Awesome! And everything turned out great, as you're a living example of.

Let's spend 30 seconds or a minute here. You brought up Ted Turner 30 minutes ago. The power of downtime and vacation time. I know that's a very important part of your life but in a very interesting way. Can you take a moment about downtime?

Three kinds of time, Dan Sullivan teaches.

You've got 'work' time, where 80% of your time is spent making money.

Then you've got 'buffer' time, where you're cleaning up your messes.

Then, the most important time curiously enough, for those of us thinking, is in our *free time*.

This means you don't take any telephone calls. You don't read any business books. You don't bring business people along.

You're not allowed to think about business for a 24-hour period from midnight to midnight, minimally.

Then, once in awhile you have to take a week off.

Then, if you take one week off, you have one breakthrough per year. Two weeks off, you'll have two breakthroughs.

I'm up to taking a week off every month right now, as is my partner. So, we have more breakthroughs.

The truth is, the Bible teaches, 'work six, take one off.' And that's cute. But, it doesn't work for those of us in thinking businesses.

For example, just real quick Mike. Your business is high stress or low stress?

I would say towards high stress.

Exactly, so you need more time off or less?

I need more time off.

And you've got to get totally away from radio when your off?

Yes.

By the way, the biggest guy ever in radio, which was Walter Cronkite, up until now. Then he went on to TV. What did he do? When he was working, he took a two week

68

hiatus. No radio. No TV. No books. Nobody with him and he went out sailing. He chilled out and he came back. And he did all the classic interviews. Like he was the last one to talk to John Kennedy before he died, and stuff like that.

That's magic. It's a miracle. How did he do it? Well, he was fresh all the time.

Let me ask this question, Mark. It's a question that I had because, a few weeks back, I interviewed Michael Gerber, who wrote *The E-Myth*.

He's a genius.

I think you and I could talk for 10 hours. But let me ask you this question: I think it's a powerful thing having a definite major purpose. I know this is a melancholy topic, but I am going to ask you anyway. Eventually, we're all going to pass on. What do you want people to say about you when your time is up?

Well, by the way, I wrote that book *Future Diary*. I said, "you ought to write down what you want on your tombstone. What do you want to be remembered for? Then write your own obituary, so that it is written right." I've done all that. On my tombstone, which I don't believe...see, all of my body parts are given away to science. Then they're going to burn the rest. With the ashes, we've told them where to go. But the headstone will say, "He served greatly, with love." By the way, that's not morbid at all. I think it's clean thinking.

That answers that question.

Who is Arthur Fry and what's the power to people listening today?

I teach a whole seminar called, "38 Ways to Make a Million A Year With Paper Businesses". It's about ideas, intellectual property businesses. Whether it's games, franchises, books, tapes, videos.

Arthur Fry is the king of intrapreneurship.

69

He found out 3M had a glue that didn't take ink off the paper. He saw the value of it when they didn't. He got 1% into perpetuity. All of us have ideas and you need to sell them to a big company like 3M that has taken 88,000 ideas and turned them into money. But his makes the most money, the little yellow 'Post It' stickies, the notes.

They make $100 million a year and he gets $1 million in his mailbox.

He doesn't care how they market it, sell it, color it, cut it.

What happens is that, he's got 29 other intrapreneurial ideas.

In other words as an entrepreneur, you take the risk, which is fun. But, it's more important to do intrapreneurial ideas.

I've got a lot of them myself so it just works. Companies will execute them for you and you just get a check in the mail every month.

Okay, we've got a minute and a half left. Someone may be listening right now with a 'poverty mentality'. They're not there yet. They want to become a success. What one simple step can they take right after the show to start moving in the right direction?

They gotta go find out who they resonate with that is super successful and apprentice to him or her for two years. Nobody gets to be a big time success who didn't apprentice. Anybody you can name, I can tell you probably who they apprenticed to because I'm pretty scholarly in biographies and autobiographies.

Well, Mark. This is the moment of the show that I hoped never would come. In all honestly, it's such a pleasure and I have such a sense of gratitude to have you on the phone.

I've been through your catalog which others can get by calling, 1-800-433-2314. Mark Victor Hanson, thank you very much!

Thank you. Have me again, Mike. Thank you.

72

Chapter Three

Conversation with Wally 'Famous' Amos

(Introduction to listeners)

You gotta be sitting down!

"Why", you ask?

Because tonight *in studio* LIVE is an individual who is a true American business legend. Why do I say that? This individual started a company based upon a food product that every single person in America has eaten and heard about. Who is this person?

Before I get to the name of this person, he's absolutely going to blow your mind for 27 fast-paced minutes, he's also the author of two fabulous books, *Watermelon Magic* and *The Man with No Name.*

He's an individual who has captivated the hearts, minds, and souls of millions of people. *Who* am I talking about?

The one and only, the *famous* one, Wally Amos.

In studio tonight to go A to Z about his life, about his companies, and about sharing true success principles with you about how you can launch your own life, your own dreams, own goals. You can find your purpose, commitment, focus. We're going to go A to Z.

If you listen to my show often then you know rule 101. Tonight *The Mike Litman Show* Rule #101 is going to be *so* important. The rule is to have a pen and paper handy because we're going to go through some *awesome* information that you need to know. Your life will never be the same!

I told you before, the man who started *Famous Amos Cookies.* The biggest and the best thing to do after the show is go out and buy some *Uncle Noname muffins*. What is that? If you're not familiar we'll get to that in a second.

We're going to go A to Z with the great Wally Amos.

It's a perfect time to start. Wally Amos welcome to *The Mike Litman Show!*

I don't know what I'm supposed to do. Or what I'm supposed to say! What *great* energy you have. I'm so wired up.

Thank you very much! It's an honor to have you in front of me for all my thousands and thousands of listeners.

Lets start where you started, the birth of your story. The Famous Amos company and the cookies that came with it that made you a household name. Tell us about the birth and the start of that company.

Famous Amos was born in 1975. March 10, 1975 in Hollywood, California. That was when I opened the very first store in the world to exclusively sell chocolate chip cookies. It just seemed that Hollywood was the place to do that. Also, I was living in Hollywood, and I learned to grow where you are planted. I couldn't start in New York cause I wasn't in New York. I was in Hollywood, California and I had this idea to just make the best-tasting chocolate chip cookie anyone has ever tasted. And to make that available to the masses and we did it on Sunset Blvd.

I mean that's fantastic. You were in Hollywood, selling the cookies. Let's stay here for a moment. You bring up that you had an *idea* and transformed it into a huge company and you lived your dream with the Famous Amos cookies!

Someone is listening right now and has an idea of their own, what steps or tips can you give them to get that idea going? To get some life to it?

74

Well, the first thing is, you got to be passionate about the idea. I'd been making cookies for five years. I'd been eating them since I was 12 years old. I love chocolate chip cookies. So, it needs to be an idea that you're in love with. That you're really married to. Not an idea just to make money with. Not an idea that you think is going to just give you material gain. Because sooner or later the passion will wear off. You won't be as involved *with* the idea, as you would if you were really in love with the idea. So, it needs to be an idea that you are passionate about.

There are some basic things that you need to do.

First of all, you need to do something!

A lot of people have ideas and they go around and they research the ideas forever. They want to get a guarantee that the idea is going to work. They want to talk to all or their friends about the idea. They want everybody else's approval on the idea before they will actually begin to implement it.

So, you got to be passionate about it. And then you've got to start somewhere with your idea.

When I had the idea to sell chocolate chip cookies one evening, I was with a friend and we decided that we were going to open a store selling chocolate chip cookies.

What do you do next? I'd *never* opened a retail store before in my life.

So the very next day, I went into the office and I said, "B.J., you know what? Call the Health Department and find out what are the requirements for opening a store selling chocolate chip cookies." Because I knew if it were food the Health Department would have something to do with it.

So, you gotta do something. You can't just sit on the idea. It doesn't have to be the beginning, the middle, or the end, but just start wherever you start.

So, have passion and take action! That's great.

Let's cover something that has happened to you over the years, I'm going to bridge into a lot of success principles that you can share. You have a great book that all my readers, all my listeners should grab. *The Man with No Name* by Wally Amos, why is that the title?

75

Man with No Name is the title because I am the man with no name! Famous Amos sued me after I left the company claiming ownership of my name and likeness, so I couldn't use my name.

You gotta have a name if you're going to have a business. Otherwise how are people going to buy your product?

So, I was walking on the beach in Laguna and actually met a total stranger. And I shared with him that I had lost the company and we were talking about another misadventure that I had actually started, called *Chip and Cookie* where I had these two little chocolate chip cookie dolls that my wife Christine created. And I was wearing a *Chip and Cookie* T-shirt as was Christine.

So, he had heard me do a radio interview and he said, "man, I heard that and it's a great idea." I said, "well it might be a great idea, but *Chip and Cookies* is sleeping right now because I'm being sued by Famous Amos." But, I said, "I'm getting ready to start another company and I was actually going to call that new company, *No Namos*. Because I'm combining no name with Amos and was bringing in the familiarity of Amos and I thought that was a hip idea." He said, "no, you know man, I think you ought to call it *Uncle Noname*." He said, "when people look at it, they are not going to say noname, even though you are going to have an accent over the "e", when people look at it they are going to read no name." That's going to be an opening. That's going to be an opportunity for you to talk about what's happening.

Well, that's exactly what did happen.

Now, an important lesson in that for me was, *listening to other people*. Because people will come up and they're going to have suggestions for you on what you should do and how you should it. Sometime you're going to listen to them, sometimes you're not. Sometimes you're going to do what they say, sometimes you're not. But you should always maybe listen because it might be something that you can use.

Let's move here for a second. There are a lot of obstacles and challenges with the Famous Amos Company that you talk about in your book. There's entrepreneurs that are listening worldwide right now. And there are successes and people who haven't gotten there yet. What are a couple core mistakes that some entrepreneurs make that you can tell them about?

Well I think the *biggest* mistake is *they don't listen.*

We become experts and we think we're experts on everything.

Now, I'm an expert on the *cookies* that I make. But I'm not a great business person. So, I think it's really important to listen. *Other* people have great ideas also. *Most* entrepreneurs don't know their limitations. When you start up a company, most people tell you that you can't do it. But then the entrepreneur says, "well, watch me and I'm going to do it."

So, you're so determined to prove to people that you can do it, that you *forget* that you are limited in many areas. So, you need to know your limitations. You need to do what you do best. It's a major mistake. The major mistake that I made was that I didn't assemble a great team of people. Because no one was there in the beginning business wise to help me put that together. So I went ahead and did it myself. And then I forgot that I didn't know what I was doing. But I kept going!

So you recommend delegating and creating a good group of people around you?

Absolutely! Which is the *hardest* thing for an entrepreneur to do because you've got this great idea and you're so passionate, you're so enthusiastic about it, you're running with the idea. You don't even want to know. And the ego gets really big in entrepreneurs. So, you gotta control your ego. You gotta listen. And you gotta *surround yourself with a great team of people.* That's the first thing I did when I put

Uncle Noname together. I got me a team of people and our company now is headquartered right here in Long Island.

What are some of the foods *Uncle Noname* makes?

We only make muffins. We make fat free muffins. There are six flavors of fat free. We have blueberry, banana, apple, chocolate, honey raisin bran, and corn. And in sugar free we make *three* flavors of sugar free muffins - multi grain, corn and chocolate.

But I've got a team of people. The president and the sales people. We've got people out in the field. So, I'm just a part of the team. I'm just a link in the chain and that's where I want to be because, ya know what "team" says, "Together Everyone Achieves More." T-E-A-M. Together everyone achieves more. So, get a good team.

That's fantastic!

(To listeners)

If you're listening right now, we're covering some *powerful,* powerful principles. Passion, teamwork, taking action, doing something now. You gotta be able to integrate and transform your life with these principles.

(Back to Wally)

I want to move here to something that is fascinating to me about the things that you have done, all the things that you are a part of. You're part of Napoleon Hill Foundation.

I'm on the board of trustees.

The great author of *Think and Grow Rich*.

Fantastic book.

Now here's my question for the great Wally Amos. *Think and Grow Rich* and Napoleon Hill transformed generations and will forever. What is the most *central* and *powerful* point that you've taken from Napoleon Hill's writings?

That's a tough question.

There's one point that Napoleon Hill suggests that I think is the core of *my* success. And that is *going the extra mile*. Doing more than is absolutely asked or expected of you. Not just doing it for benefits, for personal gain. But doing it for the benefit of everybody. The benefit of the team or the company that you work with. But doing more than is requested. Doing more than is expected of you. Going the extra mile. Giving that little bit more. Giving that little extra. It's when you're tired and you can't go anymore, then you go *even* more. Not going" well, it's not my job." But if someone asks you do to something, do it. *Or* do it *before* they ask you. That's *really* what going the extra mile is.

In *The Man with No Name*, a great book, you mentioned that you created a personal mission statement. Is that something that you recommend everybody should do?

Oh, no question. I'm a member of Unity, which is a spiritual organization. They publish *The Daily Word*. I was reading one of the Unity publications called *Unity*, which is a monthly publication. And in it the writer was talking about how people always write *Unity* and say, 'why don't you do this, and why don't you do that.' And he says, "Well, cause we're guided by our mission statement." And writer suggested that individuals create their own mission statement.

I was on my way to Honolulu. It was 1988. I was like 30,000 feet in the air. I said, "that's a great idea." And I *wrote* my mission statement. Now, it's been *revised* several times since then.

So you can be flexible with that?

79

Oh, absolutely. I've gotten it down, it's condensed. My personal mission statement is simply *to help people feel better about themselves*.

Fantastic.
Simple. Basic. But very powerful.

Absolutely, man. Because you know, I think that self-esteem is at the core of everything. If you feel good about *you*, then you're motivated, you're inspired, you've got a good attitude. You're going to go out and find the things that you need to move your life forward. If you *don't* feel good about you, then you're sitting around thinking, "oh I can't do this. Oh, look at him. They are great and they are doing all that stuff, but I can't do any of that."

PMA. Positive Mental Attitude.

Positive Mental Attitude. So my mission is *to help people feel better about themselves.*

You're well known for your promotional efforts. Being a fantastic self-promoter of things you believe in. I have people out there: entrepreneurs, business people, sales people out there. And some are shy to promote themselves. Some don't know *how* to promote themselves. What kind of tips, strategies, keys, or suggestions on self-promotion can you give them?

Well, first of all, to move off the dime, if *you* don't promote your business, who will? If you don't have the confidence, the belief in *you* and *your business* why should anybody else promote you?
So, *you* are the best promoter for your business. You have *created* this business. You know the ins and outs of this business. Go out and *promote it*. Look for fundraisers. Look for ways to get involved in the community. I don't know what your product is, but if you can *give* your product away,

80

if you can make people *familiar* with your product by sampling your product, by using your services, or using your products in some way, *that's* the way to do it. Hook up with non-profit groups.

Years ago I got involved with Literacy Volunteers of America. In this community I'm very active with Literacy Volunteers. When you can *align* yourself with a non-profit organization in your community, you then *really* become a part of that community. *Look for ways to do that.*

Fantastic!

In *The Man with No Name*, you talk about the power of visualization in your own life. Can you expand on the power of that concept - visualization?

Visualization, imagination, imaging it's all the same. We *underestimate* and *underrate* the power of visualizing what it is that we want. But you do it *everyday*. When you get up in the morning, you *think* about what you're going to wear *before* you get dressed. *That's visualization.* You can't have something in your life without first imaging it. Everybody says, "I'll believe it when I see it." No, no, no, *you'll see it when you believe it.* You will see it when you can image it, when you can begin to visualize it because what you are doing is you are feeding an image to your self conscious. And it is your self conscious that produces the results, and the material things that come into your life. So, practice being quiet, practice concentrating. When I put Famous Amos together I saw the whole thing. It was like a saw a little blueprint up on the wall. I saw each step that I was going to take. That's part of *planning* it out. That's part of *projecting* what it is that you want in life. *Use* your imagination. *Use* visualization. *See* yourself doing it. Before I give a talk, I see *myself* on stage giving a lecture. I really do! I'll give a talk before the regular talk and sometimes the talk before the talk is better than the talk. But, it's really important to see yourself going through the process of life as you're planning it, as you're doing things.

81

Ok, let's move here to something in your book. It's very powerful. A lot of times people let their past hurt their future. A lot of things that have happened sometime way back, in family or whatever, and they'll let it hurt and hindered their progress. Someone who is listening right now, and that's the case. What kind of tips can you give them to go past those obstacles and to close down their past negatives to go for future positives?

Well, understand first of all the past, yesterday, they are simply words. There is no such *place* as the past. There is no such *place* as yesterday. It's not a *place* you can actually physically go visit. The only way you can *be* there is in your mind.

So, if there's something negative that has happened to you and you want to forget it, then work on *purging* it from your mind. *Replace that with something positive. Replace that with something that you want.* Get involved in some activities that are going to be beneficial to you, that are going to be worthwhile, that you enjoy doing, that you're passionate about. Because *whatever has happened in the past it can only come back and haunt you if you bring it back.* It will not jump into your life without your permission.

You've got to let it back in.

You have to let it back in. It can't get in unless you let it in.

So, lock up the past. Steel trap. Talk about visualization. Imagine this giant steel door that just went *BAM* on your past. It's gone.

The only time that exists is right now. There is no tomorrow. As soon as you get to 12:00:01, it's today. It's always today. Whatever you want to do, you can do today. If you're not doing what you want to do today, then you are never going to do it because there is only today. There is only this second. There is only right now. Give all the positive energy, all your love, all the attention you can to do what you want right now and your life is going to be great.

That's very, very powerful!

(To listeners)

If you're listening right now you gotta be listening to Wally Amos and taking it and digesting this information.

(Back to Wally)

I want to go here. In your lectures and your books you talk a lot about the laws of the universe. *Joy* and *fulfillment*. Can you expand on the concept of using the universe? It's a very abstract concept, but using what you call *the laws of the universe*. What are they?

One is, and perhaps the most important, is that *the universe always says yes*. The universe is a *friendly* place. When you talk of the universe, we're talking of life. We're talking of every area of your life. *Life is a positive experience*. Life is whatever *you* say it is. The universe always says, "yes." It says, "yes", to whatever you say. If you say, "I can do this", the universe says, "yes you can." If you say, "I can't do this", the universe says, "yes you can." So the universe supports you in whatever *you* say. So that's tremendous power that *you're* in charge of your life through your believe system, through your thoughts. That's how you tap in to the universe. By what you believe. By being positive. By being *consistently* positive. By moving forward. By *doing* things. By being *active*. Life is not negative. Life is whatever *you* say it is. Whatever happens to you, you've got to remember that *you're* the projector. Just as when you go to a movie that image that's up on the screen, if you want to change the image that you're seeing you can't go up to the screen and pull it off.

Inside then outside?

Absolutely. It's that projector that's projecting the picture on the screen. So, *you* are the projector in life. And you are projecting through your thoughts, through your ideas,

83

through *your* belief system. *That's* why it's important to be positive.

Talk about giving and receiving. You talk about it a lot in your lectures and in your books.

Well, giving *is* receiving. People think that there's a shortage. I don't have enough of this. I don't have enough of that. But the universe is constantly reciprocating. Again, to whatever you say. If you are a giver, if you believe in sharing and supporting other causes and other people, then it's going to come back to you. It will come back to you tenfold. The Bible says that - *give and you shall receive.* That is an absolute, unequivocal truth.

The thing is that people sit around and say, "that doesn't work. I don't believe that." But they've never tried it. They have never used the principle. Listen, you don't know that one and one is two unless you get a pencil and paper and add it up and see that one and one *is* two. So, *it works if you work it.* The principle is available for everyone. It's not prejudice. There's no discrimination. It's a matter of tapping into it. It's a matter of *using* it. But, if you apply the principal, it will work in your life. There *are* universal principles. Just as there are laws of psychics and mathematics. Well, there's a way that you can live your life to be aligned *with* life. To be aligned *with* the universe. And if you begin to apply those, and *use* those in your life, you *will* get the desired results. There's no way around it!

Ask and you shall receive.

Ask and you shall receive.

Seek and you shall find.

(To listeners)

If you're listening right now you have to go out and grab *The Man No Name* and *Watermelon Magic*. You wanna go to your local food store and you want to DEMAND...

DEMAND!
Say, "I WANT!"

(Back to Wally)

What should they say they want?

Say, "I want Uncle Noname Muffins right now!" If they don't have them tell them to get 'em! Call us at 516-342-9636. We want you to have them. We'll help you get them. We guarantee our muffins! If you buy them and you don't like them, call us, we'll give you your money back.

Let's go over some things here. Wally Amos, what's your favorite quote?

My favorite quote. *Fear knocked at the door. Faith opened the door and there was no one there. What you fear does not exist. You're constantly making up.*
So go through your fears. *Grow* through your fears!

Powerful. Let's look at this. Are there any favorite books that you have? Anything that you'd recommend to my listeners? They're ready to go out and buy *Watermelon Magic* and *The Man With No Name*. What else do you recommend?

I recommend, I just read a book recently called *Tuesdays with Morrie*. It's by Mitch Albom.

It's a best seller.

It's a great book! It's one of the most powerful books I have ever read in my life. It's a book about how to live your life.

People are always talking about *business* and this and that. But, you know, its just life. Don't separate your life. *Establish* a set of principles. Establish a set of guidelines. A belief system that you can *use* in every area of your life. And that's the test of it. Will it work in my personal life? Will it work in my professional life? My social life?

You need to get something that's going to work everywhere.

You're always happy. You're always positive, Wally Amos. Give my listeners one tip to make them happy. How does everyone get as happy as you?

Get a kazoo! Every morning you get up you grab your kazoo and you play it! You paint watermelons on your shoes. When you put your shoes on and you see those watermelons you know it's going to be a good day because you've got happy feet!

(Both laugh)

That's absolutely fantastic!

(To listeners)

Go out and grab *Watermelon Magic, The Man With No Name,* and what get some muffins by going to your store or calling 516-342-9636

(Back to Wally)

It's been an absolute pleasure! Wally Amos, thank you for appearing on *The Mike Litman Show!*

Goodbye everybody!

[NOTE: Uncle Noname is now "Uncle Wally's" and can be found at www.unclewallys.com]

Chapter Four

Conversation with Jack Canfield

(Introduction to listeners)

Tonight my friends I'm going to give you a treat and a treasure. You're absolutely going to love it. This individual has sold over seventy million books. He's one of the best selling authors of *Chicken Soup for the Soul.* His other books include: *The Aladdin Factor, Dare to Win.* He's the nation's leading authority on self-esteem. Let's bring him on.

(To Jack)

Jack Canfield, welcome to *The Mike Litman Show!*

Hey Mike, good to be here.

Jack, I'm a huge fan of all your materials.

I'm absolutely grateful and have such a sense of appreciation to be with you on the line tonight.

I'd like to go through the smorgasbord of your books and materials like *Dare to Win, Aladdin Factor,* and *Self-Esteem and Peak Performance.*

Then we'll have time to get to Chicken Soup later on.

Self-Esteem and Peak Performance is an awesome, awesome course that just has great information.

Can you expand on the concept of self-esteem and talk about why it is so vitally important to personal growth?

Basically, what we've discovered is that self esteem is like poker chips.

If you have a lot of poker chips, and you're playing

poker, you're more willing to play without fear of losing a few.

So, if I've got about 100 poker chips and you've got 10, and we're playing the same game, with the same level of skill, if you bet 10 chips and lose, you're out of the game. If I bet 10 chips and lose, I've still got 90 chips left.

What we want to do is have our self-esteem level high, so that we're willing to risk.

For example, when it comes to sales, I have to be willing to risk in terms of asking for the order. If I'm in a quality circle meeting, I have to be willing to risk by sharing my point of view. If I'm not willing to go out and ask for venture capital, then I can't be as successful as some one who is willing to take those risks.

So the self-esteem gives me the confidence to be able to survive rejection.

Ok, so the obvious next question is, how do you raise your self-esteem?

Well, that's the subject of an 8-hour seminar.

But, let's try to get a couple of points here.

The first thing is that you have to take 100% responsibility for your life.

We all grew up trying to blame somebody. Whether it was Mom, or Dad, the economy, the Republicans, the Democrats, it didn't matter who.

The problem is, when you do that you ultimately feel like you're not in control of your life.

So, when you take responsibility for your life, then you can begin to take control for the parts that aren't working.

We use a formula that says, "E + R = O."

There's an 'Event.' There's a 'Response.' And then you get an 'Outcome.'

Let's say, for example, that I said to one of your listeners, "you're the biggest idiot that I've ever met in my life."

Well, they have to respond inside when they hear that.

They might say, "my gosh, he's never even met me. How did he figure it out so fast?" In that case, their self-esteem is going to go down.

If they say, "well, Canfield doesn't even know me. I'm a really great person." Then their self-esteem is going to stay high.

What we realized is that, it's not what people say or do to you. It's not what the economy does. It's not what your boss does. It's not what your children do. It's what YOU do in response to what they're doing that produces your outcome.

Let me give you an example in business.

I had a friend during the recession a number of years ago that was a Lexus dealer. And basically he believed that it wasn't the economy, it was his response to it.

So, he decided that he has to do something different. If he kept doing the same response to the same recession, he was going to go out of business. People just weren't coming in to his dealership.

So, what he did is, he asked himself, "where are the people who can afford my car?" What he got back was the answer, 'they're at the Polo grounds, they're at the country club, and they're at the yacht bases.'

So, he would get five of his salesmen. They would get a little fleet of cars and they'd go over to local country clubs and they'd say, "who wants to drive an LS400?"

Everyone says, "sure, I'll go for a little drive."

Then he'd say, "why don't you borrow the car for a week? Take your car back to the shop. We'll make a Xerox of your driver's license so we can find you."

They'd go back in a week later when their time was up, and what do you think most people would say?

"No way. I don't want to stop driving it. I like this new car."

I'm sure every one of your listeners has had the experience of getting out of their old car, going into a new car at a dealership, test driving it, and then getting back in their old car.

91

All of a sudden your old car doesn't seem as good because you now see what a better car is like.

So, this car dealer had to do something different and not become a victim.

As a result of that, he was selling more cars during the recession than he was when he was waiting for people to come into his dealership.

Let's just stay here on risk. Because I find that the big thing for you to grow and move forward is to make yourself vulnerable.

Have you found that same factor as a critical key to moving forward?

Yes, absolutely.

We have to risk, and every time we do something that's different there are 3 areas we can risk in:

We can risk in our behavior. That's what we say and do.

We can risk in our thoughts. By thinking new thoughts.

We can risk in our imagination. By imagining new pictures.

Every time we do that, we are going to risk getting an outcome that we're not familiar with.

So, we have to risk being uncomfortable.

The thing that is keeping most people stuck, and why they don't succeed more, is that they are not willing to be uncomfortable.

It's uncomfortable to try a new behavior. Like trying a new way to go home. Or using a new sales close you've never used before on a big account.

That's because you don't know what's going to happen.

But, what we do know is that, if you keep on doing what you've always done; you're going to keep on getting what you've always gotten.

If you're not happy with what you're getting, you've got to change your behavior.

Ok. So, we've got an individual who's moving out of his comfort zone.

92

But people around him are mocking him, scolding him, and laughing at him.

How do they become so focused, or so uncomfortable in his uncomfortability, to move forward through that external pressure?

Well, there are two things you can do.

One, is to start realizing something and ask yourself, "is this really the group of people I want to be hanging around with? Are they supporting you to your next level of success?"

We talked about mastermind groups.

We talk about positive support groups.

Robert Schuler talks about possibility thinkers – people who think anything's possible.

So, one of the first things you've got to do is, decide what kind of people and influences do you want around you.

There are three kinds of influences you can have around you.

You can hang around with people, like in the office. These are people that you talk to in person.

You can be influenced by the books you read, the television shows you watch, the radio you listen to, the newspaper, the magazines you read.

Then there are the seminars that you take.

So basically, you want to start surrounding yourself and infusing yourself with positive uplifting energy like you bring to your show. Also read the latest self-help books and take the right kind of seminars.

So, the first answer to your question is to eliminate some of that negative pressure by deciding who you hang out with and what you have around you.

Number 2, is to *rehearse* in your mind at night when you're alone and in the morning when you first get up.

Rehearse what you want to do. Don't worry about what people's reactions are going to be, but instead what *your* behavior is going to be.

So, when you actually find yourself in that position in real life, you're almost unaware of what's around you.

Like, for example, a good football player is not listening to the 80,000 people in the stands. The football player is out there doing a play that they've rehearsed in their mind and on the field 50 times at practice. That's the only thing they're focusing on.

Get in the zone.

Get in the zone. Absolutely!

Let's talk about a few concepts here that are mentioned in your course *Self-Esteem and Peak Performance.*

This product I'm holding here *Self-Esteem and Peak Performance* changed my life and I know it can help anyone else too.

Let's go through one or two short concepts from *Self-Esteem and Peak Performance* the audiocassette series.

You talk about a concept, Jack, called, "Universe rewards action."

Can you expand on that?

Yes.

Basically, nothing happens until people ask.

I use a demonstration in my seminars where I hold up a $100 bill. Then I say, "if this $100 bill is available, and it is, who would want it?"

Every hand in the room goes up.

I just keep holding it there and eventually I say, "doesn't anyone really want this?"

After about a minute or two, someone gets out of their seat and comes up expecting that I'm going to hand it to them.

I won't even do that.

Eventually they have to jump up and take it out of my hand.

Then I say to the audience, "what did Phil do here differently than everybody else?"

The answer is, *he got out of his seat and he took action.*

Many people learn about affirmations, setting goals, visualizing. All that stuff, and it's all very important and powerful.

But, a good game plan without action, doesn't work.

However, even if you have a BAD game plan, but you take action you can still get a lot further ahead. Of course you need to be willing to respond to what's happening and to the feedback you're getting. But if you do those things even with a bad game plan you can still get a lot farther ahead, than a good game plan without any action.

We always say, "the universe rewards action, not thinking."

Basically, you do need to do something, because people over-think and they over-prepare.

Ok.

Very interesting.

You talk about the concept and the quote, "I am enough".

Can you expand on that?

Well, the biggest thing that stops most people from being successful is they think they are not enough of something.

They're not smart enough. They're not old enough. They're not well connected enough. They're not well dressed enough. They're not funded enough in terms of their capitalization, etc.

As long as you believe that, you are never going to take the action that you need to. Because you're going to feel that you aren't yet enough of something to take action.

The way you become *enough* is by taking action and learning from your experiences.

One of my mentors, a man named Jim Rohn, whom I'm sure you're familiar with, said, "you want to set goals that are high enough that in the process of achieving those goals, you become someone worth being."

It doesn't make a lot of difference to become a millionaire.

I've done that many times over and I can tell you that it's nice to have a house and a car that doesn't fall apart and all that.

But, what's more important is *who did I have to become* in order to become a millionaire?

I had to learn how to overcome my fears. I had to learn how to talk in front of groups. I had to learn how to plan a speech. I had to learn how to ask people that I was initially afraid of to loan me money, etc.

All of that was scary. But, when I did it and survived it, I was no longer afraid to do it in the future.

Now you can take away my house, my money, my car and everything, and it wouldn't matter.

I know how to create more of those things because of *who* I've become NOT what I *possess*.

That's very, very powerful what you've just emphasized. I'm holding here, as we speak, your catalog of products, Jack. It's absolutely the top that I've ever seen.

Of course, this catalog gives more information on *Self-Esteem and Peak Performance* for those who realize they could use it.

(To listeners)

For those listening, grab a pen and paper. Write this number down. It's 1-(800) 2-ESTEEM.

If you're surfing the web after the show, there's two websites you want to check out. One is www.jackcanfield.com

To get information on the book that's rocking America, you wanna go to www.chickensoup.com

(Back to Jack)

Jack, We've got about 11 minutes to go. The book *The Aladdin Factor,* it's the awesome best-seller co-authored by your good friend, Mark Victor Hansen.

What is the "aladdin factor"?

Well, what Mark and I found out when we would go out to teach motivational seminars is, people would write down all the notes. But, then they wouldn't go out and do anything.

So, we realized that there was something missing. The major things people were missing is that they weren't asking people for the help, assistance, support, and the funds they needed to make their dreams come true.

Now let's take a look at the story of Aladdin.

All he had to do was ask the genie for what he wanted and the genie would automatically manifest it.

What we realized was missing was this factor of people not asking.

It was the Aladdin factor.

So, in the book, we basically outlined 5 reasons people are afraid to ask.

We talked about how to ask in different arenas, how to ask at work, how to ask at home, how to ask your wife, your kids, etc. How to ask, so you can get what you want.

Just to give you an example. There's a guy who was running a program called Feed the Children.

It's an organization that feeds children all over the world.

When the Korean thing was going on he realized that there were 50,000 kids in Korea that were at risk of dying.

He had no one that would be willing to fly into North Korea because their planes were at risk.

He read *The Aladdin Factor* and he realized that he hadn't asked every airline.

So, he started asking every cargo airline and every passenger airline. Then after he got to the 39th airline, they said, "Yes. We'll fly stuff in there."

Because of that, they were able to fly over $1 million of food and stuff into North Korea and save the lives of 50,000 kids.

So, this isn't just like asking for a date. We're talking about asking at any level and getting what you want.

It's absolutely powerful because it's biblical, "Ask and you shall receive."

So, let's stay here with *The Aladdin Factor* for a second.

There are a few reasons, five or so, why people don't take action.

Let's, just focus on the main reason why people don't ask.

The first reason that people don't ask, is ignorance.
They don't know what to ask for.
They've never been taught how to ask and they don't know who to ask.
So, basically that's one of the main things.
The second reason is limiting and inaccurate beliefs that people have.
Like there's not enough. Or, if you really loved me, I wouldn't have to ask. Or, the world's not a responsive place. No one cares about my needs. If I get what I want it will really make me unhappy.
You really have to go in and bore down on some of those beliefs we picked up as a child.
The third reason is fear of rejection.
People are so afraid to look bad.
I love the salesman example.
It's where there was a salesman who was trying to get to see the President.
The woman who was the secretary said, "there's no way you can get in to see him."
So, the salesman said, "what will happen if I just walk in?"
She goes, "well, he'll throw you out."
So, the salesman thought, "what the heck. I'm out in the hall. If I go in and he throws me out, I'm back in the hall. I'm already here. It can't get worse."
So, he just walked in and said, "Mr. President, I only want one minute of your time."
The president didn't throw him out of the office.
Even if he had, so what. He was already in the hall to begin with.
So, we're afraid to look stupid. We're afraid to be humiliated. We're afraid to look like we don't know what we're doing. We're afraid to look ignorant.
So, all those fears stop us.

The fourth thing is low self-esteem.

Many of us don't feel we're worthy of getting our needs met.

Some of that comes from our childhood beliefs from our parents. It's the way we've been taught, etc.

So, if you get the self-esteem programs we're talking about, they build your self worth. So, you feel worthy of asking.

The last thing is the old man who won't ask for directions thing.

Basically, it's pride. He thinks he's supposed to already know. He doesn't want to look like he doesn't know or that he needs anything.

I was working in a major airline company where the average person I was consulting with was making $70,000 a year.

I asked them, "if you couldn't find some information that you were supposed to have, but you knew your neighbor across the hall had it, how many of you would just walk across the hall and ask for it?"

Most people said they would take at least 15 minutes to look for that information because they didn't want to look stupid.

Well, that 15 minutes might have cost you or your company a couple hundred dollars worth of time just because you didn't want to look stupid.

We talked about how the universe rewards action earlier.

It's the concept of universal law. Like, "Ask and you shall receive", etc.

Can you take a moment and just talk about the whole abstract concept of how universal law works?

Well, basically anything you put out comes back.

I like the way Deepak Chopra talks about it.

He says that there's a universal field of consciousness that we can enter through meditation and through centering exercises.

Basically when we're in that state of consciousness, we're all one, we are not alone. We are all one.

What happens is that you drop into that consciousness, you drop in intention.

Deepak says, "I want to be in the highest service to the greatest number of people today."

Mine is, "I want to help as many people as I can live their highest vision in the context of love and joy."

I'm on your show today as a way of helping people do that.

I do it with the writing I do, with the tapes I create, etc.

When we came out with *Chicken Soup for the Soul*, we wanted to be #1 in the New York Times best seller list.

Every one said it was impossible. Our publisher didn't believe it. The people at the New York Times didn't believe it.

What we did is we started to ask the Universe to help us achieve that by visualizing the goal as if it is already achieved.

So, we just started seeing our name on the top of the New York Times list.

We would meditate on that for 5 minutes a day.

We actually took the New York Times list, whited it out at the top and typed in *Chicken Soup for the Soul.*

By doing it every day, what happened was our subconscious began coming up with solutions. Ways we can sell books. Not just in bookstores, where only 7% of America ever goes. But, in delis, supermarkets, grocery stores, and even places like Shell mini marts in Michigan.

One of our biggest sales places was nail salons because women sit there for hours getting their nails done, waiting for appointments, sitting under the hair dryers.

We started selling thousands and thousands of books through nail and hair salons.

We eventually made the New York Times list and our book was on there for over a year.

So, it's more than just asking someone and saying, "will you give me money."

But, there are creative ways to ask your own subconscious, to ask God, to ask the Universe, and to ask other people.

You mention the word 'subconscious'.
I think it's probably the most powerful force in the universe.
Can you give me one or two steps or keys on how my listeners can tap into the power of their subconscious?

There's two ways to use the subconscious.
One is to *ask* the subconscious for information.
The second is to *program* the subconscious with information you want it to have.
So, let's do the first one first.
Let's say that I'm going to have a business meeting with you tomorrow. I'll be trying to sell you a contract for something.
What I want to do is, the night before I go into that meeting while I'm getting into bed, I get into a quiet place and I sit quietly.
I'd bring up an image of you, if I've met you, or if not, just your name.
I focus on your name or the image of you and then bring into my subconscious the awareness of your fears, your needs, and your wants.
So, I can get to really know you and I can almost interview you in my subconscious.
Because it's the unconscious level that we're all connected on, as I said before.
There's a part of me that knows what you fear and that knows what you want.
We're all a little bit psychic.
Most of us are not trained in that arena, but we don't have to be. We just have to ask the question.
So, we're going to come into the meeting tomorrow and I'm already playing to what I know your fears, needs and wants are, because, I've learned that through my subconscious.

101

The second thing I can do is, the subconscious is kind of like a stupid employee in a sense.

It will do anything you tell it, but you've got to tell it very specifically what you want it to do.

So, I say to my subconscious, my mind, is, 'what I want you to do is come up with three solutions to solve the problem we're having with our publisher.'

I can do that before I go to bed. I can do that in the shower, or wherever. I'll tell it, "I want you to do that before 5pm, 8pm, or whenever I want it by."

Literally the next day before 5pm I'll come up with 3 solutions.

I can also program my subconscious by visualizing the successes I want to have in every arena of my life. What do I wanna look like? How much do I want to weigh? How much do I want my income to be? What kind of car do I want?

Every day spend a few minutes visualizing those things as if you've already achieved them.

It's so amazing that if people would just do this...

I could tell you story after story of people who have tripled their income, doubled their time off, achieved weight loss that no one would ever believe is possible.

Absolutely fantastic!

We're in the last 2½ minutes.

So, I'm going to put on my two-minute warning at the end of the show.

I'll bring up a couple quick topics, so just give me 30 seconds on each.

I want to get out some books you recommend to my listeners.

Well, I love the Tom Peters books. If you're in business, the chaos books. I think those are really, really great.

I think *Dare to Win*, *Aladdin Factor*, as much as they're mine, I really think they make a real difference in people's lives.

I think if you're in the work world, *Chicken Soup for the Soul at Work* out of our series.

102

Any of the books by Jim Rohn, Dennis Waitley.

Any of the guys you have on your show.

You're really telling people every week, exposing them to people to have written 5-10 books.

Jim Rohn says, "if you read a book a week, in a year you'll have read 52 books. In ten years 520 books. You'll be in the top 1% in your field. You'll be more motivated, better educated; you'll become the leader in your field."

You've got to educate yourself if you want to become richer.

(To listeners)

If you're listening right now, *The Mike Litman Show* rule #101 is "have your pen and paper ready."

You want to get to the phone.

You want to call 1-800-2-ESTEEM, and if you are on the web checking your e-mails, there's two websites you need to check out: www.jackcanfield.com and www.chickensoup.com.

If you're listening right now, I implore you and absolutely want to inspire you and entertain you to go out and pick up *The Aladdin Factor*. It's truly an awesome, awesome book.

You want to grab *Self-Esteem and Peak Performance*. It's six tapes that will keep you awake for four nights in a row.

(Back to Jack)

We have two minutes left, Jack.

Let's spend about 15-20 seconds here and give me one or two tips about masterminding. Talk about masterminding for a moment.

I think *masterminding is one of the best-kept secrets of the rich.*

Basically, you want to get together with 5 or 6 other people who are making at least twice as much money as you are.

Tony Robbins and my partner, Mark, met one time.

Mark said, "Tony, you're making $50 million a year. I'm making $5 million, what's the difference here?"

Tony said, "Mark, do you have a mastermind group?"

He goes, "what's the most anyone in your mastermind group is making?

Mark says, "I don't know, $5 or $6 million."

So, Tony goes, "everyone in my mastermind group makes $100 million or more a year."

That's who Tony's hanging out with.

Those guys are thinking with a lot more zeros after their thoughts than most of us.

Jack, you get paid a lot of money to speak for large corporations.

What are the most powerful speaking strategies you can share with my audience?

I would say you've got to love your topics and you've got to love your audience.

If you love your topic and you spend a lot of time learning about it and you share with passion, which you talk a lot about on your show, people will get excited.

They'll get ignited, and they'll want to know what your ideas are and use them.

Let me ask you this. Leo Buscaglia, someone who really impacted me, passed away.

Do you have any thoughts or anything you learned from him during his years?

Leo taught me that no matter what's going on, you can always love.

Always go back to the love and so that's something that I always fall back on.

I never try to get into adversarial positions with anybody.

Always work out a win-win position and realize that everybody's doing the best that they can with the knowledge, the awareness, and the consciousness they have.

Wow!

This was so great, Jack.

Thank you very much for appearing on *The Mike Litman Show!*

104

105

106

Chapter Five

Conversation with Robert Allen

Tonight's show is absolutely huge. If I sound passionate, if I sound excited, it's for a big, big, big reason.

Over the last 20 years there has been an individual who has been educating people across the world on how to get financially free, a greater financial future.

In the eighties he spear-headed the real estate revolution with two NY Times Best Sellers, *Nothing Down* and *Creating Wealth.* Now in the 2,000's he's educating people with his new books. One is *Multiple Streams of Income* and tonight we're going to talk about the next piece of information. There are millions and millions of websites out there. Tonight we're going nose to nose, belly to belly, with the great Robert Allen and we'll talk about his latest blockbuster book Multiple Streams of Internet Income.

Robert Allen, in the span of 24 hours, brought in revenues over $94,000. How did he do that? We're going to go in and dissect his website LIVE in a few minutes. We'll talk about the internet. We'll talk about America's foremost millionaire-maker.

(To Robert Allen)

My dime your dance floor, Robert Allen, welcome to *The Mike Litman Show!*

Mike, it's great to be here with you and to have so many people across America, I guess your audience is all over the place, isn't it?

Worldwide, Robert.

Wow! Well, I'm looking forward to being here with you today.

Fantastic. I'm a big fan of your stuff. We're going to cross over a few bridges, cross over a few borders tonight. What I want to do first, in the first half of the show, is to lay a bedrock, a foundation of the mindset necessary to be financially successful. After that we'll go through *Multiple Streams of Internet Income.* We'll dissect MultipleStreamsofIncome.com. And we'll do a lot. Sound good?

Sounds great to me!

Sounds good. Let's talk about the surrounding theme of your last two books. The theme of having multiple streams of income. Let me ask you this first question. Why are multiple streams of income so important in today's business world?

Well, just look around you in today's economy. If you haven't planned five years ago to have 4 or 5 extra streams of income by today, then you're probably holding onto one stream of income hoping that the storm is going to blow over and not affect you. I've always believed that for safety's sake, you need multiple streams of income from a lot of different sources. And not just a regular kind of income. It has to be what I call residual income. And the definition of that is to make money while you sleep. If you're not making money while you sleep you're never going to get rich. If you're going for a paycheck you're only getting paid once for every hour that you work. I like to get paid multiple times for every hour I work, from multiple sources, and in multiple areas of my life. That's the way I set my life up.

In the last book, which is a New York Times best-seller *Multiple Streams of Income* I outlined the 10 streams of income where you can do that.

In this brand new book, which was just released this week, and as a matter of fact, you are the very first show I have ever done on this book, this brand new book. You've got the scoop on it. I've never talked about this book this way on a PR tour before. You're the first one.

Multiple Streams of Internet Income is how the ordinary person makes extraordinary money online.

You don't have to be a genius. You don't have to have a lot of money to get started. You just need to have a few secrets, which we are going to reveal for you tonight.

Sounds good. Sounds strong. You mentioned residual income. The opposite is linear income. Just explain what that is before we move forward.

Linear means you work once, you get paid once.

Residual is you work once, you get paid thousands of times.

That crazy book I wrote in 1980, it's been twenty one years ago, *Nothing Down* is the largest selling real estate book in history and the reason that I get residual income is I worked once, hard, 21 years ago and it unleashed a steady stream of income into my life ever since. The book is being sold in every bookstore in North America. I don't have to be there. I don't have to do the work to market it or to sell it. It's all done now by the bookstores all across North America.

So the real secret is for you to find a stream of income where you set yourself up for residual streams of income.

Case in point would be the guy who designed and created the battery tester being used for the Duracell battery. You've seen those little battery testers that show whether your battery works or not.

Sure have.

This is an inventor who in the 60's created the Mood Ring. It's a technology called thermogenics.

So he decided that he would take this idea to the battery testing companies, which he did, and he said, "I don't want you to pay me a fee. I just want a few pennies on every battery pack that you sell."

109

Now today, he gets millions of dollars as a result of having this little stream of income from this battery pack. He worked hard once and unleashed a steady stream of income for the rest of his life. That's residual.

Whether it's in real estate, the stock market, interest on a bank account that you have, the internet, a website that's generating money for you 24 hours a day, or whether it's information wherever you are marketing it. Whether it's network marketing or whether it's licensing. It doesn't matter. What's important is you pick an area that you really love. You focus on it and do work during the time when you're not working at your regular job. Set yourself up so that 5 years from today you're free.

Ok. So we're talking here, Robert, about long-term planning. What I want to do before we cross over and even dig deeper into residuals, into internet and other facets of your ability to create residual income is, I want to lay the bedrock. You talk a lot about having the right financial mindset, the right mental thinking. Let's just cross over briefly a few bullets, a few themes. Let's start here, let's talk about financial freedom. Einstein said, "the most powerful invention of man is compound interest." Talk about that little scope there.

Well, anybody who's listening to our program can be a millionaire on a dollar a day if you understand the power of compound interest. It just takes a dollar a day at 10% interest and in 56 years you're a millionaire.

The problem is most of us don't want to wait for 56 years. But if every one of us had put $1 away for each of our children or each of our loved ones, eventually with compound interest it makes you a millionaire.

Here's the power of $1 a day:

Let's suppose somebody puts a dollar a day away for you when you're born, the very day you're born. You go to retirement age, which is out there at 65 years. If any single person in American put away a dollar a day, this is how it would grow: at 0% interest, it would grow to about $25,000. That's if you put about a dollar away under your mattress

110

with no interest whatsoever. At 3% it would grow into about $75,000. At 5%, that same dollar a day grows into about $200,000. At 10% it grows into about $2.75 million dollars. At 15% it grows into $50 million. This is on a dollar a day. Then at 20% interest, which is very hard to do especially over long periods of time, it grows into $1 billion.

The reason I share those numbers is for you to realize that what you really need is to have your money growing into what I call wealth creation rates of return.

Most people are educated to put their money at poverty rates of return, the zero, the 3-6%. The bank has told you that you've got to be careful, you've got to be safe, "we're going to give you a government guarantee." Then they take your money and they put it at 10, 15 and 20%. They become billionaires, we become paupers. But we want to be safe, right?

The real key to wealth is to realize that in life you get to choose one of two doors. You're either going to choose the door marked "freedom" or you're going to choose the door marked "security". If you choose the door marked security, you lose both. But if you choose the door marked freedom, it doesn't mean you won't lose, it doesn't mean you won't stumble, it doesn't mean you won't lose money, it doesn't mean you won't still feel insecure. But eventually you end up having not only the freedom, but you have the security, you got both.

It starts today, it starts right now where you have to make the decision to have your money growing at high rates of return and having it flowing into your life 24 hours a day.

Whatever you choose, we will talk about a lot of ways to do it here today, but you need to make that decision today.

So I want everybody to raise their right hand. Make me a promise, "I promise that I'm going to set a goal, set my sights, to one of these days whether it's in 50 years from now or 5 years from now I'm going to be a millionaire, so help me, Bob."

That sounds good. That sounds very informative. There are listeners around the world with their right hand up.

111

Let's stay here. You talked about the decision you need to make. You talked about the difference between the transition from security to freedom. Let's briefly talk about, Robert, the 7 essential money skills. Briefly share those with my listeners.

Well, if you want to be good at money, you're going to have to be good at 7 things:

#1 is you have to be good at valuing every dollar bill, because every dollar bill is a money seed. It grows if you plant it and you fertilize it and you weed it and you hoe it. It becomes a money tree. That money tree generates money for you for the rest of your life. It's on automatic pilot.

Most people don't value the dollar bill. Therefore they throw it away. They destroy it and they don't put that money away so it can grow into a half a million, or 5 million or 10 million or whatever. So you have to value the money.

#2, the second skill you have to learn is how to control it. You have to have a system for having the money flow into your life. The most important fundamental is, do you save money every single month?

The money that flows into your life and the money that flows out of your life, is there a surplus every month?

No matter what your living expenses are, no matter what your income is, there's got to be a surplus left over. It may be the hardest thing to do but is absolutely critical for long-term wealth.

The third skill is to save the money. Not only to have money left over at the end of the month but you have to save, save it.

A friend of mine quit smoking the other day and she said to me, she bragged to me, "Bob I saved $50 this last month." I said, "well, where's the money? Where is it? Show it to me." She didn't have it. It went into her budget and she just lost it and it was gone.

She should have taken that $50, pulled it out of her life and saved it. She wouldn't even have missed it! You just quit smoking. So the point is, skill #3 is you've got to save, save it. You not only have to save it but you have to get it out of your life.

112

The fourth skill is you've got to learn how to invest your money. We were talking about that when it came to high rates of return. You gotta get your money growing at 10% or more. If it's not growing at 10% or more, you're never going to get rich. You have to have high rates of return. That means more risk and it means more knowledge on your part. You've got to do some studying. You've got to do some mentoring with people who really know what they're doing and you have to increase your rates of return in things like the stock market and bonds and investments etc., etc.

The fifth skill is what we call "making it", how to make money. This is different than investing.

To invest it is a very passive thing. I can sit behind my computer screen. I don't have to know who's on the other side of that computer screen. I don't have to persuade anybody. I don't have to sell anything in terms of a product or a service. I just push a few buttons, click here, click there, I buy, I sell, I can do it in my undershorts in the middle of the night. I don't have to talk to anybody. I can be a complete recluse, but if it comes to making serious money in terms of a living and making a living and making some real chunks of cash, you're either going to do it in real estate or you're going to do it by owning a business. Both of those are going to require different skills. It's going to require some more kinds of risk, it's going to require some more persuasion ability, it's going to require some more knowledge. That's why it's a different, separate skill than just investing your money. Making it is different. I say, "there are 10 ways to make it in the world. 10 different kinds of ways to make some serious money," which hopefully we will get to.

The sixth skill is to learn how to shield your money. Because hey, you can make a lot of money, but if you haven't shielded it from the dangers of this world, then it's going to get lost.

You have to set yourself up and today it's more difficult to protect yourself with corporations and limited family trusts and LLCs and various different secret things that you do, nothing that's illegal, nothing that's immoral, but you know if you would ask me today, well ask me, Mike, ask me if I'm a millionaire.

Are you a millionaire, Robert?

Absolutely not. And I wouldn't want to be. Now, I know where the money is and I live like a millionaire, but I do not want to be one. I don't want to have my financial statement displaying to anybody showing them that I have anything. I don't want them to know where it is. I don't want them to know who owns it. I drive a nice car and I live in a beautiful home and I have beautiful things and I might travel any-where I want, but it's all paid for by all different operations and entities because it's a dangerous world out there and you have to play that game. You have to set yourself up before you get a lot of money because you need to plan for that eventuality.

A final skill is to share it. You've got to share your money. Frankly, for me, I pay my sharing first. Out of every dollar I get in, and out of every net profit that I get in, I pay 10% right off the top. It's the first money that I spend and then I live on the rest and I save the next 10%, then I spend the rest on taxes and shelter and cars and whatever else.

Robert, let me jump in here. Talk about that first 10%. You said you give it away. Talk about why you do that.

Well, in my experience, and I've known a lot of millionaires, if you ask them behind the scenes what their spiritual beliefs are, almost all of them will tell you that they believe that it's their responsibility, or even their duty, or legacy, or their stewardship that's the word I'm looking for, stewardship, to give back a portion of what they've earned from their good fortune. And therefore, you can call it giving to others, you can call it tithing. Whatever you want to call it, based upon what spiritual persuasion you come from, but I've always found that whichever spiritual persuasion the millionaires I know, they always give very generously and it's a very strange paradox. Extremely strange because on

114

one hand they talk about the power of a dollar and how it can grow into millions, even hundreds of millions and therefore you find that wealthy people are very, very careful with their pennies. Yet on the opposite side of the coin, they give away hundreds of millions of dollars.

How can that be?

You've got to be really good at controlling the money that flows into your life because eventually it will become an enormous amount that you will be able to give away. But if you're not careful on this side of your life, you won't have anything to give away, you won't have any way you can bless future generations, so it's tithing.

Give and you shall receive.

Absolutely. Whatever you give, you get back. So I try to be as generous as I can with the various organizations that I support. My partner, Mark Victor Hansen, who's the author of *Chicken Soup of the Soul*, he and his co-author, Jack Canfield…I think you've interviewed Mark before haven't you.

I interviewed Mark and Jack. It's so funny you brought that up, I was going to say when he was on the show, he talked about prosperity in the flow, exactly what you're talking about.

The way Mark says it is, it's like the various stages of water. Water becomes ice when it's really hard and cold and that's what people are with money, they're very cold with it. They're very solid with it. But as you start to give it away, it starts to loosen up. It becomes liquid and then expands even more and then as you give more of it away, it becomes vapor. So it expands out and the more you give out, the more you expand.

In fact, the more you tap into the priming pump of the universe, because the universe is a giving universe, I know that sounds a little metaphysical, but I have proven it in my own life, when I give, I get. I get hugely. When I hold it too close to the vest, I don't get and it's all part of the belief in gratefulness and gratitude in humility frankly, because this is not your money. It comes to you, it goes from you, it's really, you know, you're not going to be around to do much good with it to tell you the truth. But if you'll learn how to give, your life will be prosperous and so will the lives of the people around you.

What I want to bring up right here. I want to stop you in your shoes right there.

(To listeners)

Multiple streams of Internet Income. This will be the last book on making money online you will ever need. We're going to jump inside Robert Allen's website, multiplestreamsofincome.com. We've going to dissect it. We're going to look at it. We're going to ask him why he does what he does. I want to make a quick point here before we go to a quick commercial. We've talking about giving. We're talking about giving money, you can receive money. If you want, you can give time, you can give energy, you can give all sorts of things and they say, "light attracts light." What you give away you get to keep and what you give away comes back.

(Back to Robert)

Robert, we're rockin', we're dis secting, we're influencing a lot of people. Let's talk about the Internet.

(To listeners)

If you're behind your computer right now, you want to go over to multiplestreamsofincome.com. Before we get to it, you talk a lot about the real ability to make money online is your marketing. Talk about that for a moment.

Well, let's look at all these dot coms that just failed. Why did that happen? It wasn't because they didn't have a lot of money. What they didn't have was a lot of smart marketing ideas.

You have to market the same way online as you do offline. You have to use the same kind of principles, the same kind of strategies. If you don't, you end up losing money. I made more money myself personally than Amazon.com has made in the last 7 years. Of course, I'm not a billionaire either. But the point I'm trying to make is neither are most of the people who work there.

Amazon.com is still losing money and I'm making money every single day on my website and so are thousands and thousands of other ordinary people. You don't have to have millions of dollars behind you. You can launch your website on pennies. It's amazing!

Let me jump in. How did you, Robert, in a 24 hour period make over $94,000?

You know. When I was first introduced to the internet about 4 years ago, I wasn't involved, frankly. I was outside all the hoopla, all the excitement.

A friend of mine did a little challenge with me, he was trying to sell me a website and it was like $6,000 for a year for this darned website and I was very skeptical about it because I wasn't sure it would be possible to make any money at all. He said, "let me come to your house and I'll show you. I'll make some money right in front of your very eyes."

He flew to my home in California. Sat on my laptop computer. Hooked us up to the internet and sent out a message to his list of people that he'd been communicating with on a little ezine that he had created. Well the first order came in, in less than 1 minute. In other words, he made some money for me right in front of my eyes. And the next hour as he was trying to sell me this website, my e-mail was just dinging order after order after order after order coming into my bank account as a result of what he was doing. He did it right in front of my nose and that really just turned me on.

I wrote him a check for $6,000 right on the spot because I really realized the power of the Internet.

117

When you send out an e-mail message to people that are on your opt in list, you can't do spam, that'll kill you. But if you do a regular list with people who really like what you're doing, it's a goldmine.

So I did a challenge with a Guthy-Renker infomercial here just a while ago and I said, "I want to see how much money I can make." So we set it up on one particular day that I would be sitting at my computer, the cameras were rolling, and I sent out a message to a list of 11,000 names. I wanted to see how much money I could make from that list in 24 hours. I thought I could make $24,000 in 24 hours. By the time the 24 hours was up, the next day, we had brought in over, well, $94,532.44 was the exact number. Within the next 6 hours we brought in another $20,000. We ended up over $115,000 in just over one day.

Most all of that was profit, it wasn't cost, it was all done with a very simple process. But it took me some time to set up. When I say I'm going to make $100,000 in one day, it sounds like too good to be true and it is. It took me 9 months to set up the website. It took me another 9 months to attract 11,516 people through a newsletter that I market on the Internet for free. People sign up for that newsletter, they get great information, every once in a while I'll include an offer for something I'm doing. That's what happened in this case, but it took me 18 months to set this thing up.

Let me jump in here right now. If you look at multiplestreamsofincome.com, what you talk about, Robert, is that your greatest asset on your website is your guestbook. Without that, you have no asset, is that right? If you look at your website, a lot of what you're doing here is a lot of free stuff on the page, why?

Well, the difference between Internet marketing and traditional marketing is that, with traditional marketing when you make an offer to somebody, it's a yes or a no. You ask them if they want it. They say, "yes", or they say, "no". And it costs you money to get that answer because you have to mail a direct mail piece or a brochure or a television ad or whatever. It's either yes or no. You know whether or not you've made money at the end of that process.

But on the Internet, it's not yes or no, it's maybe.

You have this huge lake, I call it a maybe lake, because people will come in and they'll "maybe" with you for a long time. They want to find out who you are. They want to see whether they like you or not.

If they don't like you, they're not going to give you any money. But if they do like you, over a period of time, they go from maybes to yes's. Then they slip into a different pond, which I call the yes pond. Then some of those people become whales, they buy everything you've got. I call that my whale pool.

The real secret is to attract people out of that great ocean of fish. Bring them into your maybe lake so you can get some yes's and you can get some whales. The maybe part is that you get to communicate with them by e-mail. Email is free. It doesn't cost you any money to market to them.

So here is the secret. If you really want to know the secret of the Internet it is you get to fail fast for free.

Say that again.

You get to fail fast for free. Whereas in the regular world, when you fail it costs you money to fail and it's slow. You send a letter out, it takes you weeks before you really get all the responses in, or you put an ad in the magazine. It's slow. It's expensive and you still fail.

But on the internet I can send out an e-mail message. For instance, I wanted to test one of my book titles. So I sent out a message to my e-mail list and I said, "guys, tell me what do you think about this title?" Within three hours I had received 1000 responses. Three hours later, people were telling me, "don't like this. Do like that one." Guess how much it cost me to do that? Zero.

I was able to do some very scientific market testing for free. I failed, but I failed for free. Now I failed enough for free, I get to discover what really works and then I can succeed fast for free.

119

Before we step into the notion of attracting people together to give them the ability to opt-in, are there any tips you can give somebody ordinary out there who's starting a list? Any tips on the best way to correspond with them? Is it daily? Is it weekly? Is there any information you can give them as to how to move forward in that way?

> Let's pretend you're starting from scratch, OK. You have to pick a subject. Let's pick one. What do you want to sell? Do you want to sell a product or do you want to sell a service or do you want to sell information?

Let's sell information.

> Alright. We're going to sell information which is the best thing to sell because it can be digitized and can be delivered very quickly and easily and cheaply. What kind of inform-ation would you like to sell? Would you like to sell it on health or money or...?

Let's sell it on money.

> Alright. Like everybody on the line, if you're listening, it doesn't matter what you sell, you just have to love what you sell.
>
> And you're going to acquire the information that you're going to market to other people. You can acquire that information for free. It's all on the Internet. Thousands of special reports and even books are free. You can attract and acquire and get ready to market and give away to other people for free.
>
> Now, get this point. You give it away to other people for free, but they've got to give you their email address. And when they've given you that permission to have that email address, even though you're giving away other people's free information, you now built a list of people who are interested in that subject, 100 people, 200 people, 1500 people, whatever. If you have a goal by the end of this year to attract

120

in your life 10,000 emails addresses of people who've said, "send me more information. I like it for free", without even trying to sell them. What I'm trying to tell you is 1% of those people will be willing to buy what you have.

If you put an offer in your email once a month, just once a month, 1%. And you market a $100 product. An information product. Whether it's on health, relationships, diet, money, stock market, real estate, owning your own business, marketing an Internet business, there are all different types of subjects you can select. When you give away that information for a period of time, 1% of them are really hot. They want it now. They're willing to pay for it. 1% of 10,000 is 100 people. 100 people times $100 is $10,000. You do that once a month and you're making $120,000 a year for the rest of your life.

So, you've got to plant seeds. You've gotta spend the time. You gotta spend the energy. You gotta spend the money to accumulate and to gather this traffic. Is that right?

Absolutely.

And then over time, by your free offers: a free e-book, a free autoresponder, etc. You will take a small part of them, dip them in your opt-in list and then over time come to them with offers and information that expresses value to them.

That is exactly true. However! And I haven't done this yet because I really launch on my regular PR tour on the 16th of April. What I've said to the media at that point is, "give me an hour. We'll start something from scratch. And in an hour we'll be making money in 60 minutes."

Now, how do you do that?

First of all, you've got to realize that there are people online right now. Right this very second. There are at least 60 million people online right now! And of those 60 million people who are online right this very second, you get it? Right now.

Bring it to us, Rob, we're waiting, we're hungry for it, we're anticipating…

> Some of these people, they're looking, they're searching like in the yellow pages.
> See, there's a difference between a yellow pages ad and a newspaper.
> When you read a newspaper, you're not trying to read ads. You're trying to get the news. But when you're looking in the yellow pages, what are you looking for? There is no news in the yellow pages. The only reason you go to the yellow pages is because you are hot. You want something now.
> Well, the whole dang Internet is that way. It's a huge yellow pages. Except the yellow pages are free to us. We don't have to pay huge monthly fees to the yellow page companies to do it.
> Right now 60 million people are looking for information this second.
> If I can find out how to group those people into little pools of people and communicate with them instantly, I can get an instant response right now. So, "how do you find those people?" is the next question.

Absolutely.

> There are thousands who have already done the work that I was telling you how to do.
> I told you it took me 9 months to create my ezine. To gather 11,000 names. Now we've got well over 25,000 email addresses of people who want what I have.
> So, there are thousands of ezines sent out every day. Not every one of them every single day. But in every single day there are thousands of ezines that go out to these hundreds of millions of people across the Internet.
> You could buy an ad in those ezines. You can buy a sponsorship in those ezines. You can buy a single blast in those ezines for less money than you can believe. For a single classified ad it's $40 or $50. It's not that expensive.

122

So, get me on a major talk show, and we didn't set it up for you to do this with me today but what I'm going to do is get the list of say 50 different ezines of 10 different subjects and say to whoever the talk show host happens to be, "pick a subject. What subject would you like to make money in today, right now? Ok, here's an ezine that's going to go out today on that subject. We've already made arrangements to buy an ad in that and we're going to place an ad and we're going to make money in 60 minutes."

Are you going to be selling a product there or be offering something for free? What do you expect there?

It doesn't matter. Frankly, if you want to make some money, if I want to demonstrate that you can make money in an hour, then we're going to have to sell something that's going to cost.

We have about 15 minutes left. I want to get through a lot here. Let's touch on traffic. Traffic is the key to success on the Internet. A few tips on generating traffic on someone's website.

Well, there's six ways to attract traffic to your website. And they require some major set up.

If you're going to do search engines, that's going to take some work. But the fastest way to generate traffic to your website is to go to a paid search engine, like Goto.com or sevensearch.com and bid on the top spot or the top ten spot of the search engine. The way that works is you go in and bid on the top spot. Depending on which category your product is in you can literally pay 25 cents per click or sometimes as inexpensive as 2 or 3 or 5 cents a click.

If somebody is searching for something within your subject at Goto.com and your site happens to be in the top ten they'll click through to you and you'll end up paying the search engine for that lead. But the lead is a highly qualified lead. And if your website is good enough, for example, if you go to my website at multiplestreamsofincome.com, it's a very simple site. It's really not all that fancy. It's not your

123

cnn.com. It's just 'come to the site and boom here it is, free special reports. Would you like some of those? Free weekly newsletter. Would you like that?' There's also a live tele-seminar that we talk about. In other words, it's simple. I don't want to confuse people. I want to attract them to my site and if I'm going to a paid search engine then I'll drive them to my site and when I get them to my site I want them to stay long enough for them to give me their email address.

Ok, so it's about accumulating and building an asset online which is the accumulation of thousands and tens of thousands hopefully of email addresses. Some are in the 'maybe lake.' You want to bring them over eventually, once a month or as much as we can to the 'yes pool.'

(To listeners)

Multiple Streams of Internet Income. Listen to me listeners worldwide. I interview some of the biggest people out there. You know that. When it comes to the Internet and making money online you need to get this book! You need to go to Robert's website multiplestreamsofincome.com and throw in your email address. Get in the newsletter, right into his ezine and daily, weekly, monthly, etc. you'll get information. One of the great things about Robert's ezine is he brings to you some of the biggest names out there in other areas that come to you with great information. It's all at multiplestreamsofincome.com

(Back to Robert)

You talk about the ethical bribe, which leads into the power of reciprocity. What is an ethical bribe?

Well, that's when you give something and expect something in return. People are used to that. You go into a cookie store. They're going to give you a free sample. So, if you give something for free then basically people like that. And the more you give for free, the better it is. People will eventually reciprocate with you. They'll eventually pay you back for your giving. And on the Internet, it's the most powerful way because everybody is already conditioned to get free stuff. So you want to make your ezine or your website just chock full of free stuff.

For those of you who have really never been online before, just realize that you can get free stuff to give away to other people. You don't have to create it yourself. This is not brain surgery. This is not that difficult. Find a subject that you love yourself. Something that when you go into a bookstore you go into that section of the bookstore. What magazines do you take? What hobbies do you have? That's what kind of information you want to give them for free. And eventually they come to you with something you offer to them at a paid price.

Ok, let's jump in here, Robert, talk about the ability to use and what are affiliate programs?

Affiliate programs are where you sell other people's stuff.

For instance, on my website I've got an affiliate program. When people sell my stuff, I pay them. When attendees go to some of my advanced expensive seminars, then the people who are affiliates who brought those attendees to me, I pay them handsomely for that. But there are thousands of affiliate programs on the Internet. You go to affiliates.com, associate-it.com, that's the directory of associate programs.

For instance, the amazon.com website, if you put their link on your website and somebody clicks through from your website to them, then they'll pay you a royalty or a fee for that. In other words, you end up selling other people's stuff and making money from it.

So, it should be part or one of the streams of income that you're making from your website. There are six of them. #1 you should be doing joint ventures with other people on your product. #2 you should be doing affiliate programs on other people's products. #3 you should have your own bookstore where you're selling information on your website. #4 you should be selling advertising on your website. Eventually you're going to have enough eyeballs come by your website

125

where people will pay you for the privilege. If you have an ezine that goes out on a regular basis, you can charge people money for including their advertising in your ezine. #5 you should have ways of making money from what I call the infrastructure of the Internet or another way of saying picks and shovels. You want to attract people who are neophytes to the Internet business and show them how to become successful at it. This is where you can market information or services on your website about that. And #6 you should have your own auction. Auctions are wild! They're incredible! Auctions are an excellent way for you to drive traffic to your website. You should be going to Ebay and a lot of the other auction sites, putting up your information, your ideas, your products online available on auction. Give people the option to go to your website rather than waiting out three or four day auction. A lot of people just want what you have. They'll go right from there to your website and buy what you have.

Those are the six major ways you are going to make money from your website.

The most important way, obviously, is to have an ezine where you send out regular information.

One guy that I interviewed for the book lives in Mississippi. 10 years ago he was in a mental institution for manic depression. Today he makes about $15,000 to $20,000 a month. He works out of his home. He sells information on how to do wire sculpture. That's his website, wire-sculpture.com. He sells a kit for $1500 on how he took 10 years to become successful selling wire sculpture. People buy his kits. Then he sends out a regular ezine on a weekly basis and makes thousands of thousands of dollars a week as a result of that.

OK, let's stay here. Let me bring this together. We're talking about finding your passion. Finding things you enjoy. Putting it together. Starting a basic website. Accumulating information you can give for free. Getting the opt-in list going. And then communicating value to your list to people that are "maybes". Over time they'll become "yes's". It's a process and we're giving you the information more deeply, more thoroughly. *Multiple Streams of Internet Income* will walk you through it.

We've got about 7 minutes to go, Robert. I want to touch here. There are people out there who want to start simple websites. And I want to give them the best advantage possible in making it work. Talk about the power of the USP, what it is, and why it is so critical especially for the ordinary business's success?

Well, you have to be different somehow.

Let's take some of the greatest names in business. Let's take Volvo for instance. What are they famous for? When you think of Volvo there's a word that just pops in there automatically. It's "safety".

What do you think of when you think of Domino's pizza? Of course those of you outside the U.S. wouldn't think of this. But Domino's pizza's "fast, hot pizza".

When you think of something like Federal Express, what do they think of? You think "overnight". You think "the very next day".

What do they think of when they think of your product or your service?

When they think of me, most people think of "making money". You're the guy that's going to show them how to make money. Traditionally, originally, they thought of "real estate". That was my specialty. But I branched out into the stock market and the Internet and making money lots of different ways. So it's, "making money fast. Becoming a millionaire fast."

You have to have a hook, something that's your niche. The word "USP" stands for unique selling proposition. I've taken the word "USP" and I've made it into another USP word.

The U in the USP, for me, stands for an Ultimate advantage, why is your product, service or information that much better? What advantage does somebody get out of you rather than anybody else that they can go through on the Internet?

The S in the USP is, what's your offer? You need to have a Sensational offer. My offer for my newsletter for my

127

protégé program that I teach is you're going to be working with millionaires. "At the end of the year, we want you to be well on your way to becoming a millionaire." That's a sensational offer.

The P stands for Powerful promise. The promise of this internet book is you're going to be making money in 60 minutes. That's a powerful promise. The powerful promise of my *Nothing Down* book is you're going to be making money starting with nothing.

And I did these challenges where I said, "Send me to any city. Take away my wallet. Give me a $100 bill and in 72 hours I'll buy an excellent piece of real estate using none of my own money." That was my promise. We did it. We bought 7 properties within 72 hours with an L.A. Times reporter by my side.

So what do you have as your Ultimate advantage as your Sensational offer and as your Powerful promise?

Let me jump in here, Robert. We've got 5 minutes to go. I want to bring out a few things to you and let's just spend 30 – 45 seconds on them. I know you're a mentor to millions of people worldwide. You have your Protégé program people can learn more about at multiplestreamsofincome.com. Talk about the power of a mentor in general for being a success in business.

You know I've been talking about the importance of mentors for many years.

When I sat down to write this Internet book, I actually created the Foreword of it where I went through my entire life one afternoon. And I counted up how many mentors I had. And at every very important stage of my life there was a mentor there that I either stumbled onto or sought out. There are over 30 of them. 30 individual people, men and women, who had taken me to the next level.

The guy who showed me real estate investing was a multi-millionaire. I could have gone to a university for 50 years and never learned what he taught me in 6 months.

The lady who got me into publishing was a best selling author. She took me to the book seller's convention where there were 2000 publishers and she introduced me to the presidents of the companies. Now that was a massively important mentoring.

So it's important for you, whoever you are, to be mentored, to be mentored with people around you, and for you to seek out the mentors of people around you.

There's a saying that says that, "your income is the average of your ten best friends." Which means that if you add up their 10 incomes, that's about how much you're making on average. If you want to double your income, you want to triple your income, quadruple and ten times your income, you need mentors who are making that kind of income to bring up your average.

Robert, I'm jumping in right here. We've got one minute left to go. Give my listeners worldwide a few books they can read. A few books that might have influenced you that they can go out to the bookstore and pick up. They're going to go out and buy *Multiple Streams of Internet Income* today. What are some other books that you've been heavily influenced by?

Influence by Dr. Robert Cialdini.

I interviewed him, Robert!

Yeah, he's fantastic! Of course Tony Robbins books and tapes are all wonderful.

Did *Think and Grow Rich* influence you a lot?

Oh yes! Big time! That's #1 on my list! There's *The Richest Man in Babylon.*

You're a millionaire many times over, what's the biggest thing you took out of *Think and Grow Rich*?

That I could do it. It was possible. And I hope today, if you all will listen very carefully, you can do this. You can! If you have dreams, desires, goals and passions, you can do

129

this. The tools are there for you. I hope that *Multiple Streams of Internet Income* will help you, too.

Robert, thank you very much for appearing on *The Mike Litman Show*.

Alright Mike! Thank you and have a great day!

NOTE: If you're interested in starting or building your own highly-profitable Internet business, then we recommend you immediately go to: www.CashFlowWizards.com

132

Chapter Six

Conversation with Sharon Lechter

(Introduction to listeners)

Tonight LIVE on *The Mike Litman Show* we're going to bring on someone in a moment who is towering the Wall Street Journal, NY Times, USA Today. She's the co-author of one of the blockbuster books of the millenium. One of the greatest books ever on business, getting yourself moving forward, and having wealth and riches and assets. The name of the book, own it, *Rich Dad, Poor Dad What the Rich Teach Their Kids About Money, That the Poor & Middle Class Do Not!*

We're going to go on a smorgasbord. We're going to take a journey. A walk through the *Rich Dad, Poor Dad* series. Four books so far. More on the way.

We're rolling, stomping, shakin', bakin', crossing over borders and boundaries like no one's done before. *Rich Dad, Poor Dad. Rich Dad's Guide to Investing. The Cashflow Quadrant. Rich Kid, Smart Kid.* It's a revolution. It's information that can change your life.

(To Sharon)

Sharon Lechter, my dime, your dance floor, welcome to *The Mike Litman Show.*

Thank you, Mike. You are a terrific supporter. I appreciate it.

You're very welcome.

We've got so much to talk about. This is a special 57 minute edition of *The Mike Litman Show* where we're talking about the *Rich Dad, Poor Dad* series.

What I want to do off the bat, is I want to talk about the *Rich Dad, Poor Dad* story.

What I want to know is, why is it so important that millions of people worldwide hear it?

I think the best way to attack that is to explain that *Rich Dad, Poor Dad* is a very simple story of Robert Kiyosaki when he was a young man.

He had two fathers. There was his biological father and his best friend's father. The difference between those two dads is what it's all about.

His biological father was the head of education for the state of Hawaii. He always told Robert to study hard and get good grades so you can get a good job. I bet all your listeners have heard that a time or two themselves. I have.

His 'rich dad', who was his best friend's father, had to drop out of school at the age of 8 years to take over the company business and help his family.

So, he didn't have the education. He didn't have the benefit of a college degree.

But, he learned about money. He learned the power of money. He learned financial literacy.

He went on to become one of the wealthiest men in Hawaii.

Why was that?

It was because he understood money.

Robert's real dad was the head of education, but he died a very poor man.

Let's do this. You talked a little about the story of Robert Kiyosaki.

But, let's stay here. You mentioned the word "financial literacy". Can you tell us what that is and why it's so important in moving someone forward in a financial way?

Absolutely.

Well, you know you hear the story about 'reading' literacy. We need to teach our kids how to read. It's so important.

134

Well, we also need to understand numbers. We need to be able to read numbers. Numbers tell you a story.

Your report card in school had letters or numbers on it. It told you how you were doing.

In real life, you don't get a report card. But, you have a financial statement.

Your financial statement is your report card in real life.

Ok, so, we're talking about financial statements. We're talking about your report card in life.

What I want to do right now is devour and go into the book, *Rich Dad, Poor Dad*. In it you'll find 6 lessons that can transform someone's mind and someone's business.

Sharon, let's start from the lesson in the book where you guys talk about the lesson called, "The rich don't work for money." In this chapter there is a specific line that talks about how the poor and the middle class work for money. But, the rich have money work for them.

What does that all mean?

Well, let's talk about the different kinds of income that you can make.

You can make earned income, you can make passive income, and you can make portfolio income.

Earned income is what we all hear about. That's a job. That's a paycheck. That's money that you received through your own hard work. Your labor as an employee, or as a self-employed person. That's earned income.

It's very hard to get rich when your income is based on your personal efforts. You only have so many hours in the day. You only have so many days in the week.

Passive and portfolio income come from assets.

The rich know how to convert their earned income, if they have it, into assets that will generate passive and portfolio income.

So, they have their money work hard for them, instead of them working hard for money.

135

You brought up assets. Assets and liabilities are the cornerstone or the foundation of the series. Define for us what an asset and a liability is, and how they relate to someone's portfolio.

> Absolutely, Mike. I'm glad you asked.
> As you may know I'm a CPA by schooling. So, some of my fellow accountants may jump up and down in disagreement when they hear this, but it's very simple. An asset puts money in your pocket. A liability takes money out of your pocket.
> You should look at your whole financial life that way.
> Assets are things that generate income for you.
> Liabilities are things that you have to sit down and write a check for every month.

Ok. So, what we're saying here is assets bring it in. Assets is cashflow or 'inflow'.

Liabilities are 'outflow'.

I want to bring up something right away.

We talked earlier about the difference between a rich dad and a poor dad. The poor dad doesn't have as much capital and stuff going on. What is the cause of the poor dad mindset? Where does that all come from?

> Well, you said the word, Mike, mindset. It's all a mindset.
> Let's talk a little about Robert's rich dad and his poor dad.
> His poor dad constantly said, "I can't afford that."
> Saying stuff like that closed his mind to possibility.
> In contrast, his rich dad would say, "*How* CAN I afford it?"
> His poor dad didn't want to talk about money at the dinner table. His thinking was, "Do you think money grow on trees? I can't do this. I can't afford this."
> Whereas his rich dad would say, "HOW can we create this asset to pay for things?"
> If I want a luxury, I need to buy an asset that will generate the revenue to pay for the luxury. It's all in how your attitude and how your mindset is related to money.

136

Ok, let's stay here on mindset. You said something very interesting. You said, 'your assets buy your luxuries.'

Most people have their earned income buy their luxuries. Is that right?

> Absolutely!
> And once it's gone, it's gone.
> If you want a new car, you can just go out and write a check to buy your new car. But, when that car is gone, then that money and the car are both gone.
> So, let's just tweak it a little bit.
> Instead you go out and you write that same check and you buy a duplex or a four-plex. It's a piece of real estate that generates cash flow every month. Then you can use that positive cash flow to buy your car. And when that car is old and rundown and tired and you need to get rid of the car, guess what, you still have your asset. It's still generating revenue. You still have that real estate generating cashflow.

Ok, I want to make this very clear. So, Sharon, you're saying to invest in assets not in liabilities. Don't create more expenses but instead grow a cornucopia or a single property, or whatever it is that can produce money for you on a monthly basis. Then with that cashflow coming in over time, you can then use that cashflow to buy your luxuries.

What I want to do here is get into a controversial point on the subject of assets. I want to drill into my listener's heads right now that there is a contrast between assets and liabilities.

Answer this question, Sharon, is my home, is your home, is somebody else's home an asset or a liability?

> So glad you asked that question, Mike. 'It depends' is the answer. Let's talk about your house. Is this the house you're living in?

Let's take that as the example, yes.

So, it's your house that you're living in. Let's talk about the definition of an asset. An asset puts money in your pocket. Does your house put money in your pocket each month?

NO.

Ok, let's look at the definition of a liability. A liability takes money out of your pocket. Does your house take money out of your pocket every month?

Absolutely.

Exactly. You have to pay the bank. You have to pay the government through real estate taxes. You have to pay for the yard upkeep and electricity.

So, in rich dad's definition, "assets put money in your pocket. Liabilities take money out of your pockets." Which one is your house?

It's a liability.

Ok, so let me ask you this. If a mortgage is paid off in someone's home, they think they own it. They think it's an asset. Is it still a liability?

Well, let me ask you this. If you don't pay those real estate taxes, are you still going to own that home down the road?

No, I'm not.

So, there are always real estate taxes. The government is always going to have a role in that.

So, it's all a frame of mind.

We love our homes. We like big houses. But, we have assets that pay for it.

See, as an investor, you need to look at your home and ask, "what does it cost you each month?"

Certainly my fellow accounts like to say, "well, yes. You buy a home and it appreciates in value." Well, could it not just as likely depreciate in value?

You may own a home and you may sell it 10 years down the road. Maybe it did increase in value. For example, maybe you buy it for $100,000 and then in 10 years you sell it for $200,000. You would then have an asset that has put money in your pocket. But, for those ten years up until that point, what did you have?

A liability.

A liability. Because you had to generate that revenue to upkeep that house.

Let's do this. We're rockin' and rollin'. We're shakin' and bakin'. We're talking about assets and liabilities.

What I want to sort out here is a vision, Sharon. Let's create a vision, a picture. So somebody listening right now can further understand this stuff.

What does a financially literate person look like? What is the things that they do on a daily basis?

It's easy. Money and numbers tell a story. If you can just tell the story and read the financial statements, you have the ability to become wealthy.

Ok, so it's about numbers and understanding the income statements. Is that right?

Well, let's talk about the cash flow patterns of the poor, middle class and the rich.

The cash flow pattern of a poor person, what do they do? They get a paycheck and they pay their expenses every month and hope that they have a little something left at the end of the day, right?

Many times they don't. They can barely make it paycheck to paycheck.

139

So, if you're looking at their financial statements, the income comes in and goes right back out as the expenses go out. They have no assets. They have very few liabilities because they don't have enough credit to get any debt.

Then you have the cash flow pattern of the middle class.

Cash flow pattern of the middle class goes like this. Boy meets girl. They get married. Then they buy a house. They have this beautiful house, but then they have a mortgage. Then they buy a car.

They have jobs. So, the money comes in from the jobs. A lot of it goes out in the expenses. And then they start acquiring debt: mortgage, car payments, none of that money goes into the asset column. It's all in liability.

So, they have to continue working and working harder. Because, of course, when they get a pay raise, they buy a bigger house. They get a bigger car, etc.

So, the cashflow pattern of the middle class is like this: money comes in through wages (i.e. earned income) and goes out through expenses and liabilities.

Ok, I want to do something before we talk about the cashflow pattern of the rich.

I think you're talking about the proverbial 'rat race', is that correct?

I think that is a very good term.

So, let's do this. Someone's in this rat race. Someone is in the picture you just described.

If they want to take a first step out of that seat and start taking the steps toward wealth, towards riches, what can they do?

There are many things that they can start doing, Mike. I want your listeners to understand that if I make a suggestion, it is one of many, many things that they could do.

Each person has to make the determination that is right for themselves.

140

It depends on their own situation. If you have a high mortgage and you can barely make your payments, you're struggling and can't make it from paycheck to paycheck, then you need to get some advice.

You need to get some professional advice from a financial planner.

Maybe your option is to sell your home and get into a smaller home so you can start putting some money out of your cashflow into assets, into the asset column.

Or, maybe what you need to do is start a part-time business. Keep your day job. Get that paycheck. But, start generating an extra couple hundred dollars a month in a part-time business.

You might find that part-time business is going to allow you to quit your daytime job later on.

Or, maybe what you can find is, a way to generate just a little extra revenue and start looking for a piece of property. A piece of real estate to buy. A rental property that can start helping you with your cashflow.

There are many different things you can do. But, it's not the same answer for every individual. You have to choose what's right for you.

Right. So, we're looking for a mental mindset change, increasing our ability to see possibilities, taking actions steps toward assets, and decreasing our liabilities.

You mentioned starting a part-time business and doing something like that. A big part of the book you guys talk about is something called, 'mind your own business.'

Why is that so important? Is there any other way toward financial freedom, but minding your own business at some level?

Let's define mind your own business. What do you think that means, Mike?

Owning a business.

Owning a business? Ok, well, let's see. Here's how I think of minding your own business. If you're an employee,

141

what are you doing during the day? From 8 o'clock to 5 o'clock you're getting a paycheck. You're minding their business. It's what you do when you get that paycheck at the end of the day on that second Friday that matters most.

Every other Friday you get a paycheck handed to you. What you *do* with that paycheck is when you're minding your own business. In other words it's how you handle your personal financial statement. You are the CEO of your own life. That is minding your own business. It's minding your own asset column.

Many of us operate out of our checkbooks. We don't even have the concept of assets in our minds.

If you don't start thinking about assets, how can you start acquiring them?

Ok, so it's a change. A shift from just wasting that paycheck, to minding my own business and planting that paycheck like a seed, in a way that will produce a harvest for me as time goes on.

Absolutely and everybody can do it! You can start small. It's your power of choice. Every time you get your paycheck, you have the choice as to what to do with that money. It's your business and you have to mind your own business.

Because many of us are throwing our earned income into things that don't give us anything back in assets. So, the rat race goes and goes and goes.

So, would it be smart, Sharon, for someone who wants to start some type of part-time business to start educating themselves? Maybe start looking inward for a passion or something they might be interested in? Is that something you guys recommend, in a way, is to start some type of part-time business?

Education is the key, Mike. You said it exactly right. You've got to educate yourself. You can't just wait for a hot tip. So many people try to do that. It's about education and experience.

142

I know your listeners can relate to this. In school, I was a good student. But, there was always only one right answer. When you take a test in school, you were either right or wrong. You'd know what your grade was. But, all of a sudden, you're out in real life and there are no pre-determined right answers. You have to find the answer that is right for you, and that's what it's all about.

So, start making those choices. Make that choice every time you get your paycheck. Are you going to buy an asset or are you going to buy a liability?

Ok, so I want to do this. We're about 15-20 minutes in. We're talking about assets. We're talking about liabilities.

(To listeners)

I have to say right now, we're talking about something called cash flow. Where is your cash flowing? After our 57 minutes are up, you want to think about that. You want to go out there and you want to buy *Rich Dad, Poor Dad*. You want to go visit *Richdad.com*. There are three other books. There are four total books in the next thirty days that you are going to own. Why? Because you cannot afford not to own them.

(Back to Sharon)

I want to touch on something, Sharon. In the books you talk about "the rich invent money." What does that mean and how do they do it?

The rich invent money. What on earth does that mean? Well, let's say I find a piece of property that's distressed. I find a rental house. The people are desperate to sell it. So, I can pick it up at a discount. Maybe it's a $150,000 value home that I can get for $120,000. Then I have the ability to turn that around and sell it for $150,000. I've just created $30,000 worth of money, haven't I? Now, let's talk about another opportunity to invent money. Let's talk about Bill Gates. Do you think he invented some money?

143

He invented a lot of money!

> Let's look at the corner grocery store that didn't exist 5 years ago. If it's successful, the owner of that business has created and invented money. He or she has created and built a business and generated value from their own efforts and their marketing ability.

Ok, so they took an idea, they laid out a plan, established a vision, fought through the adversity and accomplished something that is producing cash flow for them.

> It is an asset. They have created an asset. They've invented it from nothing.

Let's talk about the ability to recognize an opportunity. In the books, you guys mentioned that you can't see the opportunity with your eyes, it's a mental thing. Is that correct?

> Absolutely. How many times have you heard of some-thing new, a new product or something, and your mind goes, "I could have thought of that, I could have done that." I bet all of your listeners have had something like that come along. Let's take the pet rock for example. We all have the *ability* to spot opportunities that are right around the corner. But, are we *trained* to recognize them? We have the ability, but unless you have the education and the experience, you're not going to recognize them.

The second book in the series is *Cashflow Quadrant*. Sharon, what does the title mean?

> It's Rich Dad's Cash Flow Quadrant.
> Early on in Robert's life his rich dad explained to him that there are four different kinds of people in the world of money: "E" stands for employee. "S" stands for self-employed. "B" stands for business owner, and "I" stands for investor.

Let's just take a moment and think about that. Think of the money that you have coming into your life each month. Where does the majority of that money come from? If all of your money comes in as an employee, you have a job. That is your livelihood. You exist because of that job. Your entire life depends on your employer. Is that correct?

That is correct.

If you're an "S", you're self-employed. So, you own a job. This could be anybody who is an attorney, an accountant, a small mom and pop store.

Self employed individuals love to do it their own way. They own a job. If they leave, the business goes down.

A "B" is a business owner. If you're a "B", you own a system and people work for you.

Sometimes there's a fine line between that "S" and the "B". There are a lot of people out there who think they're "B"s. But, they need to ask themselves this question, "can they leave their business for a year and come back and find it stronger and healthier than when they left?" Quite a thought.

That's something to think about. I'm going into *systems* and more "B" in a moment. Tell us about the "I".

The "I" is the *investor*. That's where your money works for you.

Now, can't you be in all four? Absolutely. Right now I operate out of all four. I'm an employee of our company, *Cashflow Technologies*. I run the company. I'm an "S" because I write books with Robert. I'm a "B" because we own the company, and I'm an "I" because I invest the money that I have into assets that also generate revenue for me.

So, you don't want to be just one or the other. You need to be all of them.

If you're an "E", great. That's wonderful. We need "E's". We aren't saying not to be an employee. But you need to take control of your own financial destiny. How can you do

145

that? By becoming an "I" or a "B".

We recommend you start as a B. Do a part-time business on the side. You'll get incredible skills. You'll learn the ability to read financial statements and then invest in assets and become an Investor.

I see one of the best parts in becoming a "B" is the transformation of the mindset. It's when someone goes from being on the poor dad side to the rich dad side. Would you agree with that?

Absolutely!

To make sure everyone is up to speed, let me explain this part of the Cash flow Quadrant. The "E" and the "S" are on the left side of the quadrant. The "B" and "I" are on the right side.

Let's just talk about it for a second, because school prepares you for what? School prepares you to be an employee or self employed. What prepares you to be a "B" and an "I"?

Maybe business school.

Hopefully our products will help prepare you for the right side of the quadrant.

But, on the left side is financial security as an employee or self-employed person. The difference is in the words that they use. An employee says, "how much do I get paid? What are the benefits? What's my vacation time?"

An "S" says, "I charge by the hour. I charge $150 an hour. I get paid 6% commission." That's the *language* used by the "E" and the "S".

On the "B" side, a "B" is going to be heard saying things like, "I need to find a new president for my company. I need to look and find good advisors. I need assistance. It's a team effort."

People on the right side of the quadrant are a *team process*, not a solo process.

An investor is going to be saying, "what is my rate of return? What is my cash on cash return? How fast do I get my money out of this project? What is my exit plan?"

It's all in the thought process and the words that you use.

So, Sharon, the beginning process from the left to the right, a lot of it depends on educating yourself and learning how to make that transition and not only how to make it, but then how to make it work. Is that right?

Absolutely!
It's totally a mindset!
One of the things we have, in addition to our books, is our game *Cash Flow*.
It is an experience. A learning opportunity for people to learn the vocabulary.
You have to learn the vocabulary of the right side of the quadrant to be able to be successful on the right side.
You need to understand what people are saying to you and this game helps you learn the concept of building assets, the concept of understanding financial statements.
We talked in the first segment about the cash flow pattern of a poor person and the cash flow pattern of a middle class person. Let's talk about the cash flow pattern of a rich person.
They have no job.
Well, how do you do that?
Think of an asset column just completely loaded. They own stocks, companies, and real estate. Those assets are generating income that flow up into the income statements.
So, what happens? They don't ever have to get out of bed if they don't want to. Their assets are generating their revenues. You know what they're doing? They're still getting out of bed every day, because every morning they're making that choice to be rich.

Ok, it's a choice to be rich. A choice which encompasses and combines and develops, which *is* the mindset!

Let's stay here, because you're mentioning the *Cashflow* game. You're mentioning *words* and *language*. You also mention something that is very interesting in *Cashflow Quadrant*. You talk about how it doesn't take money to make money. We're told that throughout our lives. What does that mean? What does it take to make money then?

Well, would you assume that you had to have money to make money?

Yes, you would assume that.

You would assume that, OK.
Well, let's talk a little bit about Colonel Sanders in the late 60s. He had a fried chicken recipe. Did it take him money to make money? No, he had an idea. He had an idea. Then he was able to find a system to wrap around that idea.
What happens is, if you have the experience and the education, the money will come. That's what we're trying to get people to understand.
The first step is education.
We are not a get rich quick company. We are a "you have the power to take control of your own financial life" company. Every one of your listeners has that ability. If they make the choice, they can learn financial literacy. They can start making that choice every single day.

(To listeners)

The best place to start it. Listen very closely. *Richdad.com, Rich Dad, Poor Dad, Cashflow Quadrant. Rich Dad's Guide to Investing, Rich Kid Smart Kid.* That's a lot. Maybe I said it too fast. You get my point.

(Back to Sharon)

Let's talk about the cash flow patterns of the rich. There's something so important, so simple, so basic, but so powerful in nature that the rich do that nobody else does. Sharon, talk about the power of tax advantages and corporations.

Believe it or not, the government is there to help you. *(Laughs)*

Get out of here, Sharon. Come on, stop joking, the whole world is listening!

(Laughing) As an employee, what happens when you get your check? They've already taken out the government's piece, right? Taxes. It's gone. It's withheld from your income.

As a business owner, you have income coming in the door. You have the ability to spend the money against your expenses. You can spend every penny of it and then, at the end of the day, you report your revenue to the government and you don't have to pay income tax if you have spent the money and proven it was spent on your business and on your business expenses.

There are legitimate business expenses out there that employees do not have the ability to take advantage of because they are W-2 wage earners.

Start a business on the side and you can actually start deducting those business expenses as long as it is a legitimate business purpose and those business expenses are related to that business. The government allows you to deduct those expenses. The rich know that.

The rich understand the ability to utilize the structure of a corporation in order to reduce their tax basis and to protect their assets as well.

So, what we're seeing here is, in the rich cash flow pattern, Sharon, we're seeing them building assets. Their asset column, the income column skyrocketing.

And what we're seeing from the poor and middle class is earned income leaving through liabilities and through expenses. Is that true?

That's absolutely right. Many of the rich *do* have earned income.

So, what are they doing?

They're taking earned income and converting it into assets that generate passive and portfolio income.

If you have assets that are portfolio, for instance capital gains, that's not taxed at 50%, that's taxed at 20%.

In many cases, if you have passive income, most of it is from real estate.

Real estate may never be taxed. It's deferred almost indefinitely because you can roll over the gain in one property into another property.

You have the ability to offset your income with something called depreciation. So, you may actually be able to almost eliminate your tax in the area of real estate.

Talk about passive income. You mention real estate. What other ways can some one achieve and draw from passive income?

Ok, let's say Mike Litman has a radio station, and he has revenue generated by that radio station. You own it. You have trademarks and you have the ability to take your radio show and syndicate it across the country. What's that called?

Passive income. BINGO – BINGO.

I want to jump back to *Rich Dad, Poor Dad* for 90 seconds, because there's something so vitally key to the millions of people out there on the left hand side of the quadrant.

This is revolutionary, this is hypnotizing, this is mesmerizing. Listen, "you work to learn, you don't work for money?" Come on, Sharon, what does that mean?

You work to learn. It's all about education and experience.

I'll tell you a little story about Robert Kiyosaki, my partner. He's only had one job in his life and that was with the Xerox Corporation.

He took that job to learn to sell.

Everybody needs to be able to sell themselves, their

150

ideas, their products and that was what he did.

If you want to experience wealth, you need to have skills. You need to have education. Maybe do it through books or playing games or videos. But, if you need particular skills, go out and work in that area and learn that skill so that you can start minding your own business. Your own financial destiny. Your own financial future.

It seems like the first transition you can make is when you get that earned income, don't be so quick, don't have your finger on the gun to go out immediately and lay it toward the expense column. If people listening could make that one transition from listening tonight, that would be a huge success. I'm really getting it that this is like a first distinction we could all make.

Let' s talk about the concept of risk. The concept of handling risk and why understanding risk is such a big way to go from the left side to the right side. Is that right?

Oh, absolutely!

It's so interesting that people say, "investing is risky." We almost laugh because to us, NOT investing is risky.

If your only source of income is from a job and your employer decides to sell the company, that's pretty risky, isn't it?

Our definition of risk is allowing your financial destiny to be under someone else's control.

Take control of your own life.

Sometimes people feel so overwhelmed by the information, and we say, "just start small." But, the issue is to *start*.

We talk about getting three piggy banks and every day put a dollar, just a dollar in each one of those piggy banks. One for charity. One for investing, and one for savings. Do it consistently every day. At the end of the month, take that charity and give it away. Take the savings, put it in a good secure short-term investment. Then take the investing money and remember, what's in that investing piggy bank. Every dollar is an employee for you. Put that in your asset column. Buy an investment and never take it out of your asset column. Every dollar in one of your assets is an employee working for you.

That is very interesting because it's *habit*, it's *action begets action*. It's doing things. It's creating *momentum* and it's creating a different energy in your life. Is that right?

I couldn't have said it better myself.

Let's talk about your definition in the context of what is "wealth"? When someone is *wealthy*, what does that mean?

I'm so glad you asked. This is my favorite.
People say, ok, the definition of wealth…they start immediately thinking of a dollar sign and numbers.
Our definition of wealth is measured in *time*. That's right, *time*. If you lost your job today, how many days forward could you survive based on your assets?
Now many of your listeners may be rolling their eyes in panic and fear.
It is exactly that. If you have assets generating enough income to cover your monthly expenses, you are independently wealthy. Infinite. Because you could quit your job tomorrow and maintain your style of living.
Many of us, unfortunately, if we lost our jobs, may only have 2-3 months of money in our account. Our wealth is measured in time, not in dollars.

Ok, we are getting a lot of e-mail questions. I want to get to a few.

Jason in California wrote, and I'm paraphrasing, to get that question out to you.

At your company *Cashflow Technologies*, you, Robert and your people are a great team.

You guys talk about the power of teams.

If you're starting a business, what should you look for in people, is there some criteria, is there some characteristics of something you

152

can do to form a good team. What do you look for?

> You want a shared purpose and a shared mission. You need a mentor. You need somebody who has been successful in the arena you are in.
> But don't just go up and ask, *will you be my mentor?*
> There is something called *the power of exchange.* Do something to help *them* and they will help you.
> Many successful people love to share their success and help others become successful. But, be respectful of their time. That helps.
> Go to local association meetings and start networking. Networking is an incredibly powerful tool.
> Start asking other successful business people, "Who are your accountants? Who are your tax advisors? Who are your attorneys?"
> You'll start getting a network of advisors.
> Business and investing is a team sport. You need that advice.
> Can you imagine trying to do everything on your own against the rest of the world?

That's an S, right?

> That's an S.

(To listeners)

Ok, *Rich Dad, Poor Dad, Cashflow Quadrant*. There are two more babies in my hand and there are a bunch of babies on the way. The next 30 days, I'm telling you, make the sacrifice, and it's not a sacrifice at all once you get the book. Own all four of these books. Your next present, buy the *Cashflow* Game.

Start changing your words. Start changing your habits. Start changing the thinking.

(Back to Sharon)

Let's go into *Rich Dads' Guide to Investing* for a moment as our journey continues and let's talk about investing. Let's talk about the power of using your current earned income to create passive and portfolio income.

Somebody out there is saying, "Hmm, I'd love to get into the "I"." What are some of the things they can do to begin to look at the "I" quadrant?

> Let's talk about it. What kind of investments are there in the "I" quadrant?
> People say, "well, I have a savings account."
> But, is that an investment or is that savings?
> We differentiate between savings and investments.
> Investments take the shape of several different formats: Real Estate, hard assets, that's an investment. Building a business. That's an investment. Creating products. Selling those products. That's an investment. Also, buying and selling stocks, that's an investment.
> You have to choose the right investment for you or the right blend.

Let's talk about the idea of planning for investments and the concept of an *entrance* and an *exit strategy.*

> Well, investing is a plan, Mike.
> That's what's so important for people to understand.
> You can't just say, "I'm going to become an investor."
> Investing is a plan. You need to choose a formula, master the formula. It may take 5 years to master the formula, but it's methodical. It is a calculated decision that you make every day to follow a plan for investing in your own personal financial future. That choice is personal to you.
> Now, when I talk about investing as a plan, there are different types of financial plans. Everybody needs a financial plan to be secure. Everybody wants security. The rich, they have secure plans. Then you want a plan to be comfortable, maybe you want to take that three week vacation every year, you want to be able to retire a little earlier.

So, you have a plan for *security*. Then you have a plan for *comfort* and a third plan is the plan to be *rich*. That's where you look at having money that will support you in a lifestyle that you choose to be in.

We're talking here, Sharon, you're talking really about the mindset again. The way of thinking. The way of acting.

I have question here from Troy out of Utah. He is a small business owner and he wants to look into the corporation. What is his best option out of the gate? Is it an S-corporation or a C-corporation and why?

Well, that's another very good question, and unless I know his specific issues, it would be very imprudent for me to make a decision over the telephone like this.

Ok, so answer this question. What *is* an S-corporation and what is a C-corporation? What's the difference?

An S-corporation is provided by the tax law to allow you to have the protection, the *liability* protection of a regular corporation, but the income passes through to your personal return. So, you have the ability to only be taxed at your individual rate.

Now, a C-corporation is a separate entity. With a C-Corp, you and your tax return are separate from the corporation. The corporation has its own identity and its own tax return and has got its own set of rates.

Many times people say, "Oh, it's so difficult to have a C corporation. You have compliance. You have double taxation." But, those are all things that can be managed through education and understanding and through proper advice from your legal and tax counsel.

Troy may have a small business that generates $100,000 a year and the S-corporation form may be perfect for him.

But, he may be taking that small corner operation and franchising it across the country. He may want to be able to provide fringe benefits to his employees that may only be available through a C-corporation.

For him, he needs to know what his own plan is. What his goals are. What his future is, and then get proper advice as to which entity is best for him.

Sharon, talk about the concept of being, doing and then having. You're reversing everything that we think we know. What does "be-do-have" mean?

Well, it's one of my favorite formulas because it's such a simple formula, and yet in order to *be* like a rich person, you have to learn what the rich people know.

You have to *be* a rich person in your mind. It's that mindset.

Then you *do* what the rich do. We've given you the formula. We've shown you the things that they do and it's a very simple formula that we follow.

You do that, then you can *have* what the rich have.

So many people try to start at the end. They get the job. They go out and they buy the Mercedes. They buy the big house. They jump over the be-do-have, right to the have and then what they have is yes, all those fancy toys, but a *lot* of debts, a lot of *liabilities*. They buy liabilities that they think are assets.

Let's repeat that – they buy liabilities that they think are assets.

That's exactly correct, Mike.

(To listeners)

OK, we're on our fourth step in the journey.

"The fourth step," you think, "how many steps can Mike take tonight?"

Rich Dad, Poor Dad. Cashflow Quadrant. Rich Dad's Guide to Investing.

For every parent listening today, now there's *Rich Kid, Smart Kid*, the newest blockbuster out of the gate from the great people at

(Back to Sharon)

What is *Rich Kid, Smart Kid* all about?

All kids are born rich and born smart. That's our philosophy.

You have the ability, as a parent, to help your child learn and become financially literate.

The sooner you start, the sooner they will win.

The world is changing. But, our education system hasn't been keeping pace and I know everybody's nodding right now. We are in the information age, our educational system is not teaching us what we need to know.

How many of your listeners were taught about money while in school? Not many.

This book was written, really, because Robert, himself, was a frustrated student.

He hated school. He hated it.

He didn't learn in a traditional way.

I have three children and as a parent I know that each of my children learn differently.

So, what we have is one educational system.

It's a great system, if your child learns the way that they teach.

Unfortunately there are many kids out there who need experiential learning. They need to be able to draw, touch, feel, experience.

And in order to be successful in today's world, they need to learn about money.

Money is a life skill.

We teach our kids about vitamins. We teach them about exercise, but we don't teach them about money.

Whether your child's going to be a janitor, CEO, President, real estate investor, whatever their choice in life is, you still have to learn how to deal with money.

It is a life skill.

It's our desire and our goal and our mission to be able to provide the information for parents who want to help their children learn financial literacy at a young age.

(To the listeners)

Ok, if you're a parent listening right now, I'm holding in my hands right now, *Rich Kid, Smart Kid*. Own it.

(Back to Sharon)

What's an action step towards the process of education and financial literacy from a parent to a kid?

It's awareness. It's vocabulary. It's being aware of the world around you.

Letting your children understand that they are geniuses. Support your child. Talk to them about money.

Let them see you pay your bills. Talk to them when you go to McDonalds.

There are some financial field trips in the back of the book that actually helps guide you through it.

Your child will build an awareness. There's a company that only makes straws for McDonalds. There's another company that only provides the signs, the golden arches.

It's an awareness of the world around them and the fact that there are many, many ways to make money and create businesses.

Sharon, I'm instituting my two-minute warning. We've got five minutes to go, I'm going to throw a few things at you, we'll be brief, to the point, and we'll move forward. Sound good?

Absolutely.

People around the world are going to seminars with Robert, with you, all over the world, from Australia to Maine, from everywhere. I've got an e-mail from some one here and people have really fallen in love with Robert Kiyosaki.

Tell us a little bit about who he is and the man he is from your perspective.

Robert is an incredible communicator.

He has the ability to take a complex subject, like accounting and finance and financial statements, and explain them in easy to understand, simple formats using pictures, using examples, and storytelling.

He is a master communicator and he is a gift.

His products, his education is a gift. People are just blessed by it. We are blessed by the response we get from it.

I have accountants who call me and say I really got it, I thought I knew this stuff, but I really understand it now, because you explain the very simple basic formats.

(To listeners)

OK. *Rich Dad, Poor Dad.* You say, "Mike, I know where to go, *Richdad.com.*" Get the book.

(Back to Sharon)

You talk about the B-I triangle. It's very interesting.

What exactly is the B-I triangle and what is the meaning of it?

The B-I triangle is a plan.

If you want to be able to build your own business, whether it be a piece of real estate, a rental property, an entire multi-million dollar Fortune 500 company, or a corner hotdog stand, you still have basic elements.

You need the team.

You need leadership

You need a mission. Your mission is all important.

Those things are all on the outside of the B-I triangle.

Then the B-I triangle has five different tiers. Those tiers are all systems within a successful company. They're all inter-related.

The bottom one, of course, what would you think that would be?

Earned income? I'm not sure to be honest with you.

159

The bottom one is cash flow management, Mike. (laughs)

You're not supposed to ask the host those questions. (laughs)

(Laughing) *Cash-flow management.* It's like oxygen. Blood to the body.

Any business just like with individuals. It doesn't matter who you are. You need to be able to understand money. Cashflow management.

The next one above that is *communications.* You need to know how to talk to your customers. You need to be able to communicate to the world that you're there and you have a business. You also need to able to communicate with your employees internally. You need to be able to communicate with your investors.

Then there's the *systems management.* Every company is a system of systems and if your systems break down, your company implodes. You may have a huge successful product and not be able to make enough to meet demands. What's going to happen? Your company may fail. You haven't built the systems to support it through.

Sharon, I got the next one to redeem myself. *Legal management,* tell us about it.

Yes sir, the legal stuff. People say, "oh my God, lawyers." But, there are good lawyers out there, too.

Intellectual property. You may be able to protect your ideas from other people utilizing them. You may be able to prevent barriers of entry of other people. You may be able to protect your share of the market, because you properly protected your idea. And that's very important.

Also, make sure you have good agreements with the people that are doing work for you so they don't steal the idea.

Legal is a very important part.

People say, "I don't have the money to afford attorneys, it's too expensive." But, many times they find out it's much

160

more expensive if they don't.

Sharon, let me jump in. Take us down the road in 30 seconds. What's up next for Rich Dad's products?

Rich Dad's advisor series. We are introducing it here tonight. This is my first introduction, on your show.
Rich Dad's Advisors are going to be released in June of this year.
We've brought in the people who have helped us. It's our team and we are sharing their expertise so that your listeners and our readers can know what questions to ask and how to find their own team of good financial advisors, of good legal advisors, of good tax advisors. To help them create their own financial plan to become financially free.

Sharon, we're wrapping down the show. Thank you for coming on *The Mike Litman Show!*

Mike, thank you! You're terrific.

162

Chapter Seven

Conversation with Michael Gerber

I have to tell you right off the bat. I'm excited tonight! Why am I so excited? Why is my passion coming through the microphone? Listen very, very closely. Because tonight is a special edition of my show. "Why?" you ask. Because *in studio* LIVE tonight we have an individual who has an absolute underground best seller. It's sold hundreds of thousands of copies. The book, *The E-Myth*. This book and this author are creating an absolute revolution across the fruity plains. It's geared toward small businesses and home businesses. Changing lives, changing businesses.

And I have to tell you this...In bookstores right now, the next soon to be best seller by this individual called *The E-Myth Manager*. An absolute awesome book geared toward the manager. *The E-Myth* is geared toward the entrepreneur in you.

What we're going to talk about is, what is "the e-myth"? "The e-myth manager"? What's an "e-myth consultant"? What's "*The E-myth Academy*"?

I know you want more. I know you're interested. You want information on Michael Gerber and *The E-Myth*. Let's cut right to the chase.

(To Michael)

Michael Gerber, welcome to *The Mike Litman Show!*

Hi, Mike.

People all over the world are fascinated by *The E-Myth*. But there are people out there who say, "Michael, what is the e-myth?"

Can you just go right to the chase, what exactly is "the e-myth"?

> The e-myth is the entrepreneurial myth. And essentially what it says, is that most people who go into business aren't entrepreneurs as everybody says they are, but what I've come to call 'technicians' suffering from an entrepreneurial seizure. So Mike, everybody goes to work in their business, creating a job for themselves. And it suddenly becomes the worst job in the world because they're working for a lunatic.

Who's that lunatic?

> The lunatic is us. Mike, everybody who owns a business - doing it, doing it, doing it - busy, busy, busy, knocking their brains out 12, 15, 18 hours a day. They go home. They can't sleep. They get up in the middle of the night. They got to go back. They got to do the work. They got to make it, sell it, ship it, do it. They can't think of anything else and the sucker doesn't work. They do.
> So the problem with small businesses is, the businesses don't work, the people who own them do. And they're doing the wrong work.

Okay, let's take a step back before we go forward.
What's fascinating about things that you talk about is the true purpose of business. Why should an individual be in business? Can you go a little step further and explain the concept of how somebody can properly use their business to enhance their lives?

> *The real purpose for creating a business is to sell it.* So in other words, if somebody wants to start a business, the very first thing they've got to ask themselves is, "how do I get rid of it?" Most people who own and operate their own businesses, Mike, haven't the faintest idea how they are going to eventually get rid of that business. They haven't started it as an entrepreneur does. An entrepreneur is already *thinking* about when they are going to sell their business. They're going to go public. They're going to *find* a

164

buyer. They're going to *find* the capital they need to expand it, to replicate it, to grow it, to take it worldwide or whatever. Most people don't do that.

Wow! That's really interesting. And we look at rates of businesses today. 95% of businesses go *out* of business. Eight out of ten businesses fail. And the franchise concept, which we will get to soon, succeeds.

Let's take a step back here. So technicians start businesses. But let me ask this, what is a technician?

Well a technician is somebody who has done something. They fix cars. They sell something. They make something. They do something. In other words they are people who do it, do it, do it every day and they're doing it for somebody else. So they're working for the boss and one day some of them wake up and say, "What am I doing this for? Anybody can run a business. Any *dummy* can do this. I'm working for one. Why don't I do this for me?"

So the auto repair guy, the mechanic, decides to open up an auto repair business. And the graphic designer decides to open up a graphic design business. And the attorney decides to open up a legal practice. Each of them believing in what I call the 'fatal assumption' behind every small business out there and that is "if I understand how to do the work, I understand how to build a business that does that work." And it's absolutely 180 degrees from the truth.

Wow. So their *entry* into business is the wrong way. So let's ask this, what's the first step an entrepreneur can take? How does an entrepreneur think? What are some questions they can ask themselves to start a business the correct way?

Well, the very first question is, "What do I want?? And *not* about the business. It's not about the business. Business is a *boring* thing. You've got to understand, you know, I call it "C.O.D." It's your crap out date. You are going to die. Every single, I'm 61, so understand *mortality* is the

165

issue. I'm gonna live and I'm gonna die. And every single second we stay here doing this we're getting closer to C.O.D.

So the real question isn't, "what business do I want to be in?" The real, first, very most important question I talk about in *The E-Myth* is, "What's my primary aim? What's my vision for the *life* that I want to live in order to get what I *really* wish to get while I'm here?"

That question, Michael, that you just said, '*What do I want my business to accomplish for my life?*' is a very unique question. Would it be correct to say that the reason why small businesses fail all across America is because *their entry into business is totally corrupt?*

Yes. Their entry into business is totally corrupt. They started for the wrong reason. They started "to get rid of the boss." And then they *become* their own boss and as I said earlier, "they're working for a lunatic." They are busy, busy, busy, busy knocking their brains out doing every last unimportant thing in that company, that in fact, is exactly the *opposite* of what they need to do.

Okay, let's do this. We've painted a picture. *The E-Myth*. The picture of the entrepreneurial myth in America. But somebody is listening right now and saying, "Michael, give me an example. Make it clearer to me." You talk about an instant that happened in 1952 that has changed the way I think, changed the way millions and millions of business owners think across the country. In 1952, the man with the milkshake. Can you take it from there?

Sure. We're talking about Ray Kroc. We're talking about McDonalds.

Ray Kroc was in fact the *epitome* of entrepreneurial thinking. But, of course, so is Fred Smith of Federal Express and Anita Rodick at the Body Shop.

How do those people *think* that is different from most people who start their own business? Well, Ray Kroc saw the *business* called McDonalds as his product.

Hold on. The *business* as your product?

The business is your product. The business is the entrepreneur's product. Not the hamburgers. Not the French fries. Not the milkshakes. Not the software. The *company* called MicroSoft is my product. The *company* called McDonalds is my product. The *company* called Federal Express is my product.
So Ray Kroc went to work *on* McDonalds, not *in* it. To create an absolutely impeccable turnkey *system* that would replicate the results he wanted no matter how many stores he opened up. No matter how many trucks Federal Express has got out there in the street. No matter where they are, those little suckers work in an absolutely predictable way so he can make a promise, "when you absolutely, positively *got* to get it there over night, call us. And when you don't, call the Post Office."

That's an absolute breakthrough because Ray Kroc, Fred Smith, The Body Shop, an individual named Tom Watson something in *The E-Myth* that - hold me right here...

(To listeners)

If you haven't bought *The E-Myth* go right to your bookstore.

(Back to Michael)

Tom Watson said something so interesting. We know the IBM mystique. The clothing. The processes. Tom Watson. Ray Kroc. Now, I have somebody who is listening right now who is saying, "Ray Kroc. McDonalds. But, I'm a carpet cleaner. I'm a lawyer. How do I even move forward in that type of model?" What would you say to them?

Well, what I am saying to each and every one of the

167

examples, and every other example that is out there listening to us, is essentially, what you do, the kind of work your *company* does - law work, graphic design work, contracting, it doesn't really make any difference. The *real* work is the work of the entrepreneur. The *real* work is the work of the organization. The *real* work is to create a *system through which your company can absolutely differentiate itself from every other company in the world because it's able to do what it does impeccably, infallibly, every single time.*

So, if in fact what Ray Kroc *perceived* is that, "my business is my product." Then you take it to the next step and understand *my business has got to become a brand.*

Wow! We all jumped upside down, fell on our head! A revolutionary way that successful businesses: Ray Kroc, Fred Smith.

(To listeners)

Listen. If you're listening to this show, you're in Long Island, you're in New York, you're in Australia, you have to understand. The point we want to get across is Michael Gerber and *The E-Myth* is a totally different outlook, a different aspect in your business.

We gave you a different outlook on your business. But I want to cut to something really interesting right now that is an absolute secret, an absolute technique that Ray Kroc has used. That Bill Gates uses. That Fred Smith of Federal Express uses. And if you can use this, what Michael Gerber is going to describe in a few moments, you can absolutely see a gigantic change in your business.

What am I talking about? What I am talking about that is so powerful that it could affect your business is the importance of *telling a story.*

(Back to Michael)

Michael Gerber, what is the importance of having a story to tell?

Well, the importance of having a story to tell is, that's what everybody's interested in. Everybody wants to hear a story. And what they want to hear is a great story! So *great entrepreneurs tell great stories.* And the great story is, the

168

story of my company. The story of what we do. The story of how we do it. The story of why you should connect with our company rather than with anybody else's company. And that is what every single one of the owners of those small businesses out there should be doing. They should be creating their story. Let me tell you a story. Let me tell you a story. Let me tell you a story. They should be able to tell that to people who want to come to work for them. They should be able to tell that to their banker. They should be able to tell that to the supplier. They should be able to tell that to the customer. They should be able to tell that to everybody and anybody. They should go home every night and tell the story to their kids. They should go home every night and tell the story to their wife or to their husband. To anybody and everybody. They got to practice telling the story. *Storytellers are what make the world turn 'round.*

Wow! So we have the mouses. We have the absolutely, positively service. We have just huge things.

But I have people listening: small business owners, home business owners, entrepreneurs, and they're saying, "this is revolutionary. This is a breakthrough."

How can they look at their business and what are some ideas that they can use to begin that storytelling?

Well, they need to think about their business.

(To listeners)

And hear me when I speak to everybody out there. I am speaking to you. You have to begin to ask this question, "What must my business look like and feel like when it's finally done?" Understand. Remember earlier I said, "the sole reason for creating a business is to sell it? Well, you've got to start your business *today* as though it were the very first day and you have got to ask the question, "What is my business going to look, act, and feel like when it is finally done, so that I can sell it for 20 times earnings?" How much do you want for your company? You want a million dollars? You want two million dollars? You want three million dollars? What's it got to look like in order for somebody to walk up to your door and say to you, "I'll take it. I'll take it. I'll take it"? Just like Ray Kroc's franchisee walked up to him. And Ray Kroc said, "and let me show you how the little sucker works. Let me show you how the little sucker works. *It* works so you don't have to! I'm not going to sell you a job. I'm going to sell you a *company* that can deliver on its promise over and over and over again." And the franchisee said, "I'll take it." And Ray Kroc said, "Not yet you don't. First you got to go to school." What school? Hamburger U.

You got to have a school. You got to have a way of doing what you do. And the *way* that you do what you do has got to be able to differentiate you from everybody else in your business so you can become the person that they say, "You're those guys! You're those guys who do that extraordinary thing!" And the only way you can do the extraordinary thing is if you got a system to do it! That's what Ray Kroc understood. *The system is the solution.* Not people. Not all these extraordinary people out there in the world. I'm saying that every extraordinary company discovers how to produce extraordinary results with *ordinary* people doing *ordinary* things in an extraordinary way! And the system, *the intelligent system is the leverage through which you do that*!

I guess that's so clear. Because if you look at McDonalds, it's a billion dollar company being run by people out of high school. Pressing buttons. Hitting the hamburger button. Pressing the salt. Hitting the catsup.

It's so interesting. Hamburger University, I mean, what a wacky concept! Hamburger University.

But isn't it fair to say, Michael, that people, business owners listening right now can model that same thing? That same type of training that Ray Kroc did?

That's what software is. I mean we are in the technological revolution for God's sakes! *Software is a*

170

system. Software is the *leverage* through which ordinary people can do things people could never do. The computer enables us to do calculations so much faster than we could ever even comprehend them. Software is a *system* solution to people problems. Your company *must* become your software. And understand when I say that, I don't care what you do. I don't care if you are a financial advisor. I don't care if you're a poodle clipper. I don't care if you are the most sophisticated company in the world. Intelligent systems. *Intelligent systems in the hand of ordinary people produce intelligent results.*

That's such a breakthrough! Because it's fair to say that there are businesses out there looking for the *extraordinary* person. The extraordinary person. The best resume. The highest thing from this school from that school. What you're saying is amazing! We are turning America, Michael Gerber is turning America upside down because we are so resume oriented. Resume, resume, this, this. If the system is the answer, the system is the solution, what you are saying is that, *ordinary people do extraordinary things*?

Just think about it. If that's true, and it can be verified over and over and over again in the most extraordinary companies, if that is true, then the whole *idea* that we're being told today about the knowledge worker, the whole idea that we need to become more people intensive, the whole idea that our assets go home every night, and that's the good news...I'm saying that's exactly flying in the face of the truth. The truth is counter-intuitive. The truth is, if we understood that you can create an intelligent system to do *anything*. And if you can teach somebody to learn to use that system, talk about economic expansion, talk about an economic explosion, talk about freedom! It's extraordinary!

Wow! I can vouch for this.

171

(To listeners)

If you can focus for a second, you are listening right now and you are absolutely compelled because the reason this show is on tonight is we are opening your eyes. We are turning the switch on.

I'm going to take it up a notch and turn up a few notches right here. Because there is something that you see in Michael Gerber's video, in Michael Gerber's books. You're mesmerized by the information. You're mesmerized by the energy. There's something that Michael Gerber talks about called, "the tyranny of routine."

(Back to Michael)

The tyranny of routine is such a unique concept that you talk about. Can you take it from there? What is "the tyranny of routine"?

> The tyranny of routine is what everybody experiences everyday. Every small business owner goes to work. Builds a business. It depends upon him or her. Does it, does it, does it, does it.
>
> Now they're not only doing the stuff they know how to do but they're doing all the stuff they *don't* know how to do. They're *consumed* with work. *The business runs their life. They don't run the business's life.* Their business *is* their life. Their life isn't their business.
>
> But it should be exactly the opposite. Our *life* is our business. We need to create a *life* that works. And the only way we can create a life that works is if we escape from the tyranny of routine, doing it, doing it, doing it, busy, busy, busy. And the way you escape that, is to create a turn-key intelligent system that takes care of the tyranny of routine and gives us the freedom, the liberation, that effectively keeps us from having to do it.

People listening know that I want to make some things clear. 1952. You mentioned Ray Kroc, the turn-key revolution. Just to make it clear and talking to someone who is not as up on some of the buzz words. "Turn-key revolution". Can you just explain what this is?

Turnkey revolution is the system. The system is the solution. AT&T said it. Ray Kroc said it. W. Clement Stone wrote a book years and years ago about the success system that never fails. Life is a system. The *universe* is a system. An *atom* is a system. Our *body* is a system. The *relationship* we're having right here is a system. The people who are listening out there is a system. *Everything* is a system.

The question becomes, "How do we *transcend* living in the trees to be able to grow higher than the forest, and see how we live? We have to transcend it. And when we transcend it, we end the way we live it right now.

Absolutely awesome! Absolute breakthrough!

(To listeners)

I bet you never thought you'd hear LIVE tonight from Michael Gerber, author of *The E-Myth,* the book that is just sweeping across America. You thought *The E-Myth* swept across America, you have to get ready for his new book, *The E-Myth Manager.* It's absolutely awesome.

We'll talk about E-Myth Mastery, E-Myth Academy but before that there is something that I know you want to hear. If you read *The E-Myth,* you read about some 5,000 prototypes, "cloned franchise prototypes." I have to ask the great Michael Gerber...

(Back to Michael)

Tell us about "replication", "five thousand", and "franchise prototypes".

Well, we have worked in *The E-Myth Academy* for the past 20 years with more than 15,000 small businesses. We have clients throughout the world. They are in the UK. They are in Australia. They are in New Zealand. Throughout Canada. Throughout every state in the United States. All were small businesses who were doing it, doing it, doing it, busy, busy, busy. As I have said, "consumed by the tyranny of routine." Who suddenly said, "there has got to be a better way." And the better way is going to work *on* your business, not in it. To do what? To create your franchise prototype.

So what I am saying to every single small business owner. I don't care where they are, Mike. It doesn't matter where they are. What they do. How they do it. Whether the economy is up or the economy is down. Whether they've got two people, one person, 300 people, 5,000 people. The rule is universal, absolutely universal. And it works every time somebody does it. They got to go to work *on* their business starting today to create *their* franchise prototype, *their* little turn-key system. So they could imagine replicating it *5,000 times*. They could open up 5,000 more just like it. Just like Ray Kroc did. Just like Federal Express has. Just like everybody and anybody who understands the turn-key revolution. The idea of building a *business that works* rather than going to work everyday.

Let's do this. Somebody's saying, "Ray Kroc. Fred Smith." You talk about it in some of your tapes: "McDonalds. Body Shop." Talk about this, you mention in one of your tapes, a company that cuts hair and is growing by leaps and bounds. The company is *Super-Cuts*. Have they done the exact same thing you're describing?

Exactly. In fact the guy who created SuperCuts, we had an incredible conversation. This guy was a truck driver. He was having a mid-life crisis. He went to beautician school. He learned how to cut hair. And in the process as he is doing this - he is the only guy there – he's about 6' 8", he's there with all these young women, you know, and other guys, but nobody like him. You understand? I mean this guy is a guy like you think. He's driving trucks. He's driving trucks. He's driving trucks. You see? He's in *beauty* school and he's sitting there and he's saying, "gosh, there's got to be a better way than this. There's got to be a better way than this." And so essentially what he did is, design the SuperCuts *system*. "This is how we do it here. This is how we do it here. This is who we are." And because he created the SuperCuts system, he was able to teach and hire abso-lute *novices* to cut hair. "This is how we do it here. This is

174

how we do it here." "How do *you* do it here?", is the question.

This is SO revolutionary! Because they can have SuperCuts University, model Ray Kroc. When you think about hair cutting you think, you know, the man or woman, there is a level of expertise needed. But he's taken it down to the basic science that is absolutely awesome.

Someone's listening and might say, "This is awesome. But how do I go about doing this? What are some things that I need to do?" And you talk about something you call, "innovations, modifications, and then orchestration." Can you put that in English for people listening?

I could. But let me do one thing. Essentially what the person has got to ask himself, herself, right now, as they are listening to this or when they stop listening to the radio, what they have got to ask themselves is this question, it's not my question, a guy named Barker created this question. "What's the one thing I could do that's impossible to do, but if I could do it, it would immediately transform my company?" So, that's what the SuperCuts guy asked, "What's the one thing I could do that's impossible to do, but if I could do it, it would immediately transform my business and in the process of transforming my business, transform my life?"

So, understand, this whole idea of creating an exceptional small business that does an ordinary thing, I'm talking about *any* kind of business, any kind of ordinary company, I'm not talking about whiz bang extraordinary things you got to invent. Any company. Any, any, any company sitting out there right now doing stupid stuff. "How do I do this stupid stuff in an extraordinary way?" The way I do it is to ask the impossible question. "What could I do?"

For example, a medical clinic. What happens when you go to a doctor? You wait! Right? Everybody waits. That's why you got a waiting room! So you can wait! The imposs-ible question the doctor would ask is, "how could I actually keep my appointments every single time, on time, exactly as

175

promised, every single time, or we pay for it. How could I do that?"

Any medical clinic that could do that. Mike, any *contractor* who could do that. Any *landscaper* who could do that. Any *poodle clipper* who could do that. Anybody who could do that, would absolutely seize the imagination of their customer.

Well, how do you do that?

You do it with a system.

So the way you invent that is innovation, quantification and orchestration. That was the question you asked.

So, to innovate, is to invent?

To invent a new way of doing an old thing. Not discovering a new thing that you are going to immediately do in an old way. I'm talking about an old thing in a new way. An old thing in a new way. *Fast. Clean. Guaranteed. Absolutely, positively when you want to get it there overnight.* Domino's Pizza, a pizza in 30 minutes. An old thing in a new way. That's the deal and the only way anybody can do that is with a system. An extraordinary system in the hands of ordinary people.

Domino's pizza in 30 minutes. Millions of dollars. Tom Monahan, the true guru behind the concept.

He definitely is.

It is interesting. Now, we're innovating. We're moving. Now, we are doing it, doing it, doing it, but we are doing it the right way. We're going A to Z. I'm getting there. *How* do I know it's working?

You know it's working cause it's producing results. You quantifying it. That's a good question, Mike! You quantify it!

So effectively you *find another way*, you *count* what happens, you *quantify* the impact.

176

So sales go up 14%, the minute you quantify it, guess what you do next, Mike?

Before we get to that. Before we get to what we do after quantification. Before we go to *The E-Myth Manager*. Orchestration, tell me about it.

Orchestration. Once you've innovated, once you've created a new way of doing an old thing, once you've quantified that it *absolutely* improves your productivity, the next thing you have to do is what nobody does. Orchestration.

You have to eliminate discretion. That choice at the operating level of your business. Understand. Every extraordinary guy and woman who owns an extraordinary company says one thing that nobody out there has the courage to say, "My way, or the highway. My way, or the highway."

Why?

Cause it works!

And that is what differentiates us from everybody else.

So orchestration is to create a system so if you discover something that works, everybody who does that work in your company has to do it identically the same way. And that, Mike, is called a brand. *Our* brand of business, not their brand of business. And that's what makes it so extraordinary.

What came to mind is, I go to Kinko's and do a lot of copying. Usually they wear the same clothing. They talk to you the same way. They have a brand taking the copying to the next level.

Let's do this. I've got to ask you this question, Michael Gerber. You talk about something that's called "the power point in business". What's "the power point in business" all about?

The power point in business essentially was my need to find a word that described the intense energy that exists at the center of a universe.

You can just imagine the intense energy at the center of the universe and that your company is the center of people's universe. And effectively they live it and feel it and taste it and love it and hate it or whatever the hell they do. Do you understand?

That intense experience is the power point. It is the identification that every extraordinary business has. It's the way it lives in the world. It's a brand. It's *a way of doing business that is absolutely proprietary to you*, and it works.

Awesome!

The "pragmatic idealist", you talk about. I have to ask you about it. What is the pragmatic idealist?

Pragmatic idealist is what an entrepreneur is. An entrepreneur doesn't live in a false world. I mean, we all do. We all dream. But, the pragmatic idealist suddenly says that, unless it works in the real world - pragmatic - forget it. But unless it reaches for something higher, something extraordinarily special, why bother? So that's why these extraordinary companies are so extraordinary. They are doing ordinary things, Mike, in an extraordinary way and it's because they have a *systems* perspective as opposed to 'get another guy, get another guy, get another guy'.

Can you imagine if Federal Express was just hiring fast guys?

I mean, you know, get a fast guy. Get a guy who can really do extraordinary things. Extraordinary things. I need extraordinary people.

And when they did extraordinary things, another company would pay them more money and they would go there!

Right! The assets go home every night.

You can always find an ordinary person.

Right.

178

Ordinary people doing extraordinary things.

We're all ordinary.

(To listeners)

If you are listening right now, you have to write something down right now that if you are an entrepreneur, or manager, technician, I don't care who your are, what you do, you need to read this book. Why? Awesome, awesome, awesome! The first thing you have to do right now. If you are one of four people left in America who hasn't read *The E-Myth*, I'll see you at Barnes and Noble or Borders in a few minutes.

But now, coming to your bookstores right now, is a book that I'm hitting right now and you have to buy. It's called *The E-Myth Manager - Why management doesn't work and what to do about it*. You have to get it.

(Back to Michael)

I have to ask you this Michael Gerber, *The E-Myth Manager,* take me deep inside *The E-Myth Manager* and tell me what is that all about?

Well, what it's all about is we work in so many companies, so many owners of businesses, and they start to work on their business using E-Myth Mastery, which is our extraordinarily unique program doing ordinary things in an extraordinary way. The system solution that bring expertise, business expertise to small business owners. Every single one of these thousands upon thousands upon thousands, people say, "yeah, but how do I get my manager to do it? How do I get my manager to do it?" I say to them, "you can't get your manager to do anything. You've got to discover how one becomes an extraordinary manager by learning an *extraordinary* way to do ordinary things." Most managers have never been taught how to do that, so I became so damned frustrated when people ask me that question, I finally had to say, "well, I'll tell you, I'll go write a book."

179

Now this book took me longer to write than any book I've ever written. They're called. "E-Myth books." The first book is *The E-Myth*. The second book is *The Powerpoint*. The third book is *The E-Myth Revisited*. This is *The E-Myth Manager*. And my next book, soon to be out, after *The E-Myth Manager* is digested by hundreds of millions of people, is called *Job Free*.

Hold on! I gotta stop you right there! You are going from the entrepreneur, to the manager, to job free? Sounds like the technician!

You got it!

Tell me about *Job Free*.

Job Free is the technician. In other words, how do you apply the "E-Myth" way of thinking to the owner, to the manager, and to the technician, so that each and every single one of them understands?

You're transforming businesses!

You got it!
But, the only way you can do that is by transforming the way people think. Mike, it's not about passion. It's about thinking. How to transcend the way you think.
You remember that movie, Dead Poet Society with Robin Williams? Remember what Robin Williams did, he said, "Kids, jump up on the desk. Jump up on the desk. Doesn't it look different from up here? Doesn't it look different from up here?" Doesn't your *company* look different from up here? Doesn't your *work* look different from up here?

If I remember correctly, they took some slack for that. So is it fair to say that people who hear you talk about transforming your thinking about your business, aren't some people around you going to think you are nuts or something?

Of course they do! Everybody is going to think you're nuts! Because everybody else does it the other way.

That's my point.

Everybody else is saying, "Passion, action, thinking. Passion, action, thinking." I'm saying exactly the opposite. It's all counter-intuitive, Mike. It's all exactly turning life on its ear. It's turning everything upside down. We have all been taught that if we can become passionate like we are right now. They say, "oh, my God. The reason these guys are successful is because they are so passionate." Bull! It has nothing to do with passion! It has to do with a rationale model of the universe. What universe? My universe. Your universe. This universe. That's what we have to do.

Let's do this for a second. There are people who are just going bananas! They're reading *The E-Myth. The E-Myth Manager.* They're saying, "I want to help share this passion. Share this mission. Transform businesses. Michael Gerber can only do so much." And you said, "okay." *E-Myth Mastery. E-Myth consulting.* It's sweeping America. Thousands and thousands of people are going to do the e-myth on their local businesses. Tell me about that Michael Gerber.

Well, it all starts with the idea of the company, which is *the E-myth Academy.* As I said, we've been doing this for 20 years now. The original reason for creating the *E-Myth Academy* was to create a turn-key system from which we could work with small business owners. But, at very, very low cost, as opposed to very, very high cost. I was so sick and tired of paying professionals *huge* amounts of money for stuff that if they really wanted to they could have told me in a minute. In other words, I knew, Mike, that there was a system to solving the problems that everybody out there

181

listening to us right now faces. So we created it and we did it and we did it and we did it. And the whole idea was to create a consulting system that I could put in the hands of an ordinary woman, an ordinary man who absolutely wished to have an extraordinary impact upon other people. And be able to help people to do that. So, we created *E-Myth Mastery*, which is our three-year program for implementing the E-Myth in any business. And we created E-Myth certified consulting so that I could attract people out there who want to bring the E-Myth to businesses in their town, wherever they are and we'll teach them exactly how to do it.

Ordinary people doing extraordinary things.

You got it.

I got a question here from a gentleman. His name is Matt, in Alabama. He asks, "Michael Gerber, what is the most important step an entrepreneur can take to begin setting up the system in his or her business?"

The most absolutely important thing you can do, Matt, is read *The E-Myth*. Now, if you haven't done that, you have to do that. That's the first thing.

The second thing you do once you have read *The E-Myth* is to ask yourself the question, "what do I want from my life?" Forget about your business, Matt. Forget about your business. It's a complete unadulterated waste of time. Matt, forget about your business. This is not about business. Your life is your business and so you have to ask yourself, "what do I want?" What I mean by that is, what is your primary aim? Do you remember earlier, we talked about creating a story? Telling the story. Our life is a story. The problem is everybody else is writing it. The problem is we're not writing our story. So this is the very first thing we tell our clients to do. Mike, the first thing you do when we get done tonight you go home and you imagine your C.O.D.. Imagine your crap out date. Imagine you're at your own funeral and suddenly you're speaking. You're at your own funeral. You're speaking to everybody at the funeral and you say, "listen I have to tell you a story. Nobody else could tell you this story like I can. Nobody knows me like I do." Your dead, Mike, you understand? You made the recording before C.O.D., before you died. What story would you tell them?

Okay, so today is the first day of the rest of your life. What a cliche. What a horrible cliche. But the fact of the matter is, it is!

Imagine going home tonight and writing this script for the tape you're going to play at your own funeral and saying, "Hi. I want to tell you the story of a guy. His name is Mike. He was, you know, however old when he saw the light. And that day he decided he was going to create by *intention*, absolute *intention*, the rest of his life. This is the story."

Then once you got the story, tellin' it, tellin' it, tellin' it.

Telling it, telling it, telling it, and then living it, Mike. But nobody does that. Everybody is out there having accidents.

Everybody is out there being busy, busy, busy.

Busy, busy, busy and I'm telling you if it works, they take credit for it. If it doesn't, they blame everybody else.

It such a major breakthrough! You're just turning, you know, Godzilla on his head, saying, "you want ordinary people. The system is the solution."

You got it! There is an extraordinary way to do anything. The problem is we are so focused on people. We haven't focused on the work. So we've got to ask ourselves, "but how does that work? But how does that work? But how does that work?" And as we *transcend* the experience and *watch* ourselves work, we can begin to discover a better way, and a better way, and a better way, and that is what innovation is all about.

Innovation. Quantification. Orchestration.

An individual, Terry, wanted to know something. He was passionate about *The E-Myth*. He wants to know how he can transform and get the E-Myth more in his life. How do I become a certified E-Myth consultant?

> You become a certified E-Myth consultant, first of all, by reading *The E-Myth*. If *The E-Myth* blows your mind, which it does, and if it doesn't - forget it. But if it does, then you've got to ask yourself this next question, "would I like to share *The E-Myth* with small business owners throughout the world?"
>
> Now understand this. This is a critical point. If the answer is, "yes", then you've got to become certified as an E-Myth consultant and we have a certification program, for a fee, through which we teach people who wish to deliver this E-Myth mastery program of ours to anybody, anywhere, throughout the world.
>
> So, see the neat thing is to be a certified E-Myth consultant you don't have to deliver to the guy next door. We do it online. We do it online. It's on-line consulting! Our certified E-Myth consultant has the world within his or her reach. So they can work with people anywhere. Just as we do. We've got certified E-Myth consultants in Australia working with clients in the U.K. We've got certified E-Myth consultant in the U.K. working with clients in Australia. You can work with anybody, anywhere, no matter where you are. From your home.

And bring the E-Myth message to millions upon millions of small and mid-size businesses.

> Mike, I have to add one last thing.
>
> There are three opportunities: To apply The E-Myth to your own company. To become a certified E-Myth consultant. Or, three, to actually participate in the E-Myth Manager Intensive. But you gotta call 1-800-221-0266 and

say, "I want to apply the E-Myth to my business. I want to become a certified E-Myth consultant. Or I want to become a certified E-Myth manager. Show me how. Tell me how." Or say, "I want to see Michael in person." And understand, I'm getting older, Mike. I mean, I'm getting older. I'm not going to do this for too long. I'm tired of working in it. I'm working on it. I'm working on it. I'm going out to spread my story. To tell the story to the thousands upon millions of small business owners who are waiting to be transformed and that's why I came here.

Absolutely awesome!

We've got about a minute and a half. We have to do this. We're going to go about a minute here. I want to take 20 years and bring it down to one thing. I want someone to be able to go out tomorrow and say, "this is the E-Myth. This is what I'm talking about." We've got the McDonalds. We've got the Kinko's. Give one or two things to look for in a successful business today.

A successful business works without the owner. A successful business works without the owner. *A successful business works without the owner. The E-Myth Academy* is working. God bless it. I never go in there. I'm in Long Island, it's out there working. Got people all over the world doing the work of a certified E-Myth consultant, delivering it, delivering it, telling the story and producing, Mike, you cannot believe the profound impact. It's 20 years in the making. That's how extraordinary it is!

(To listeners)

You've got to leave here with a few things.

Ordinary people doing extraordinary things. You've got to leave here realizing that the entrepreneurial myth has been almost a disease in American psychology, in American business.

What Michael is talking about here is just absolutely turning it on its head.

185

We're coming down to the end of the show. Understand that in 57 minutes even Mike Litman and Michael Gerber can't tell the whole story.

The E-Myth is the first step. I'll tell you that you want to buy *The E-Myth*. And I'll tell you that I've read the book 18 times! My book is dog-eared. This is my book, dog-eared from head to toe.

(Back to Michael)

I have to tell you Michael Gerber, *The E-Myth* has changed my life! Tonight has changed my life! And I'm just absolutely happy for my listeners to get to hear you just go A to Z, coast to coast, belly to belly, for 57 minutes. I want to say from the heart, thank you, Michael Gerber, for appearing on *The Mike Litman Show!*

Thank you.

187

188

Chapter Eight

Conversation with Jim McCann

(Introduction to listeners)

A true Long Island success story. A true New York success story.

An individual who will go down in history as someone who built one of the greatest business empires ever in Long Island.

In the last decade this individual went from social worker to owning a few florists, to having an absolute empire that does over $400 million in sales per year.

Dominates the Internet. Creates absolutely awesome relationships. I've used his company countless times.

I met him at a function. He's an awesome individual.

I'm holding in front of me over 200 pages that is the absolute must-read book of this year. One of the top five books that you need to get your hands on. Have a pen and paper handy, because *Stop and Sell the Roses* is an absolute must for any listener.

If I sound excited...If I sound passionate, it's because the individual I'm going to bring on in a moment has so much information to help you explode your business to the next level, just like he did.... You want to hear the one and only Jim McCann, the author of *Stop and Sell the Roses*. The CEO, the head honcho, the big man on campus, 1-800-FLOWERS.com servicing all your flower needs. A to Z. 1-800-FLOWERS.com, just an awesome, awesome company.

The book I am holding right now is absolutely a must own, *Stop and Sell the Roses - Lessons for Business and Life*. It's from the individual who is the head honcho of 1-800-FLOWERS.com. He's easily the Michael Jordan of the flower industry.

Let's get to the point. Jim McCann, welcome to *The Mike Litman Show.*

189

Hey, Mike…thank you for that introduction…

Jim it's an absolute pleasure. Long Island loves you, the service you provide and the jobs. Everything's awesome.

So many things about your story and an awesome book captivate my attention. We'll go through, in the time we have together, some of the book, how this all happened, what's going on today, and some tips and strategies that you can give to business owners listening.

Sure.

So, I have to know this.

Before we even get to the social work that you did which was very impactful on your life, walk us through in 1987 when you got into the flower business.1-800-FLOWERS.com. How did this all happen?

Well I've been a florist for over 20 years now, Mike.

The first 10, I had a full time job, as you referenced, my first career was in social work. I ran a home for teenage boys in Rockaway and different group homes around the area. And in doing that work, which was my primary career, it was a job that I wasn't good at to begin with. But then I became pretty good at it and developed a real passion for it. I loved the work I was involved in. It was a work that you could live and breath. I couldn't wait to get up in the morning and it totally engulfed my life. It was rewarding, Mike, in every way imaginable. It helped me grow. It helped me to learn about myself. It helped me to feel like I was making a contribution.

But the only way that it wasn't rewarding was financially. And "not for profit" social work is just for that - *not for profit.* And by that time I had married and my wife, Marylou, and I had three young children, and I needed to provide for my family in a better way than I could at that time. And they wanted to do some really strange things those kids of mine.

190

They wanted to eat. They wanted to go to school. They wanted to buy clothes.

So I was always doing things on the side.

I grew up the son of a painting contractor in Brooklyn and Queens. I grew up in that business. So I was used to working a lot and working hard. I was always involved in other things. Mostly real estate. I'd buy houses. Fix them up. I'd rent them out. I'd buy small commercial property. Always doing that on the side.

Somebody told me about a flower shop for sale.

Growing up where I did in Richmond Hill, Queens area, I always had a fascination with retail because I think retail is the true interactive commerce experience. People vote *for* you or *against* you every day, all day. How well you're doing. How good your prices are. How good your service is.

I heard about a flower shop and I thought I don't know very much about flowers. But I had time. That is, I had weekends, and why don't I work there.

So I worked there for several weekends in this one flower shop in Manhattan. And low and behold, Mike, I got hooked. I got hooked on it because it's a special kind of a business. It's a business that you don't have to worry about going out of style because it has been around since the beginning of time.

Every culture known to man has used flowers in a celebratory way since the beginning of time. So it wasn't going out of style.

It was a business that had another aspect to it that *wasn't* the business. That there was a *craft* element to it. An artistic end of the floral shop. And as a florist we get to involve ourselves in people's lives in a *very* special way every day. Whether it's all those celebratory occasions like birthdays and anniversaries, get well, new babies. We are involved with people's lives at a very special time when they are trying to make a connection. They are trying to express themselves in a special way to somebody else. Even in times of sympathy, we're involved in very emotional laden times.

191

The firestone. The explosion. How did the 1-800 number come about? What's the story behind the explosion in your life? 1-800-FLOWERS.com. How did that come about?

The 10 next years after I bought that flower shop, I became hooked on the business. I became hooked on the magic of flowers and how they impact lives and how it can be a noble and perfect profession.

And so the next stage for me was to try to expand that business. So I kept the full time job for 10 years and continued to grow my flower shop business. By that time, the rest of my family came into the business. My parents when they were alive. My brothers and sisters. And we grew to a nice little chain of 14 stores here in the New York metropolitan area.

A company was launched in 1984 called 1-800-FLOWERS out of Dallas, Texas. It was the best idea I've seen in our business and I thought that it could be marketed properly and perhaps change the way in some small degree, the flower business worked at that time.

Unfortunately, we didn't have anything to do with it except we became a fulfilling florist for this company.

To make a long story a little bit shorter, they had a grandiose plan. There were some flaws in it, the company took off like a rocket ship and came back to Earth just as quickly.

They asked if I would come run the company. I said that I wasn't interested in a job. I already had a job and, in fact, I had a couple of them.

But I did say I would be willing to buy the company. That is, in fact, what happened.

I bought what was left of the company. I changed the name of *our* company locally to 1-800-FLOWERS and then changed the way we marketed our company. And then in the next 10 years we grew 1-800-FLOWERS.com into a nationwide company.

Tell me your story. It seems like your story really is about you taking action and you taking risks. From a store, to go into flowers,

192

to seeing an opportunity in 1-800-FLOWERS.com and putting a lot of capital on the line. Can you talk to somebody just about how important action is and taking realistic risks and really moving forward in a business?

Well, one of the things is in the book that you were so nice to mention earlier that we have out in the bookstores now called *Stop and Sell the Roses* and one of the things we talk about it there is another guy who had a trademark on the term, The Ten Commandments.

So we couldn't infringe on his trademark, so what we have is the Semi-Commandments. And in fact we went with 11 because we wanted to do them one better.

One of the semi-commandments that we talk about speaks on exactly what you said. The wheel has already been invented. So you are not going to come up with anything so radically new that it's going to change the world. If you do, fine. But don't wait for it.

So what we try to say in the book is, "don't try to know everything about the business beforehand and don't worry about the fact that the wheel has already been invented."

The key ingredient for people like yourself, Mike, who are terrifically successful and the Bill Gates of this world, and all the different industries that you can point to someone who's the leader, who's the revolutionary.

Bill Gates didn't invent the operating system. Someone else wrote it, he bought it from them for $50,000 as legend would have it.

Most of the great business ideas that we have seen in the last 20 or 30 years start out as a joke. People laugh at them when the first hear them.

But the real business opportunities that have been created are done in areas that aren't particularly sexy, aren't particularly innovative, and aren't necessarily this new high tech wismo gismo.

But what they are is someone who had a *passion* for something. The key or the secret: Find something that they're interested in that gets your juices going. That you feel passionate about.

193

Mike, how many times have you seen it that the *difference* between somebody who had a good idea and someone who acted on a good idea, that the person who acted, acted. They didn't wait for everything to be lined up.

It's that simple one word - action.

What you said though, something I want to focus on right here is, you said that a lot of times when extraordinary businesses are created, people think it's a joke at first. When you were doing this whole flower thing, were there many people to the left and right of you who thought maybe you were a little nuts or what's this 1-800-FLOWERS thing?

If somebody's listening right now and they have an idea, how do they stay focused against the criticism that can come to them by people surrounding them? How do you stay so focused?

I think it goes to the test of your own commitment and your own self-image. And that is, if you think that this can happen, don't worry. If a lot of people thought it could happen, and if people just slapped themselves on the head and said, "Great idea, it's going to work," I'd have more suspicions than if people say, "Gee, I don't know if that will really work."

There is no *reward* for attorneys or accountants who are the professional who we should rely on, but we have to understand that there is no reward for them telling you, "hey there's a great idea. Take a risk." They'll tell you, "Geez, I don't know about this, you gotta consider that." It could depress you but *that's their job* and why you are paying them. And that's why they're in the professions that they're in.

They are there to *advise* you, to counsel you against the risk. But it's *your* decision to manage the thought process. It's *your* responsibility to decide whether to act or not. Not theirs.

You're saying some million dollar words. You're saying *decision, thought process, action, risk.* Some of that you have done,

194

people might look at you or talk to you and think you did this complex thing, which is very complicated. But, you took an idea, and you took action, you stayed committed to your plan until you succeeded with what you're doing now.

It doesn't mean that you jump off the end of the pier either though, Mike. I mentioned to you that I'm not a *big, big* risk taker. When I bought 1-800-FLOWERS frankly it was a big mistake. I now know what you know, and that is do your *due diligence*. I didn't know about *due diligence* at that time.

Research.

I did due *negligence*. I made a mistake. I bought a company that was severely in debt. I walked into it personally with a lot of debt. Knowing what I know now, I would have never done it that way. You *can* make mistakes. But then I had two choices. The people who are in your audience, people like yourself, Mike. The difference between those folks and the people who make mistakes and then allow it to clobber them are people who make mistakes who are entrepreneurial have *one* secret ingredient in the makeup of their character that allows them to survive those situations. And that is *they recover quickly*. That is, you make a mistake, you have a bad setback, someone you thought was very close to you or who you hired all of a sudden announces that they are leaving. Boom it hits you in the gut. It hits you in the labonza. It takes the wind out of your sails. But ten minutes later you're looking at the bright side of things. Okay, I'm going to recover this way. I'm going on with it. You dust yourself off. You pick yourself up and you get on with it.

The difference between people who make it and those who don't is the people who make it know how to recover from setbacks and recover quickly.

195

It's very interesting you bring that up because on our show we've interviewed big entrepreneurs, big authors, and it seems like some of the most successful people out there failed the most, and their ability to recover really was it.

> That doesn't mean you have to go out and look for failures.

Right. But you go out there and you do your best. You study your plan. And sometimes, as you said, you get knocked down. It's about getting up and keep going.

> Well, Mike, I'm sure you have people who call into your shows, who say, "geez, you know, I'm working this job. I'm making a living but it's not what I want." And they say, "how would I really get started in the business?" And sometimes I get frustrated with folks who say, "oh, I really would like to set up a dry cleaning business. But how do I get started?" Well, number one, you don't work 24 hours a day. You have time in the evenings. You have time on the weekends depending on what kind of shifts you work. How about getting a part time job? "Oh, it doesn't pay that much." Who cares? It's a learning experience. You think you'd like to be in that business. Work for somebody else and use that as, A) your making some spare money on the side; and B) you are doing research or learning about another industry. You're seeing if you would really like it.
> You can sample around with part time jobs. With volunteer jobs. If you say, "I think I'd like to be an off premises caterer." Then work for somebody. Work as a bartender, or bus boy, set-up person, equipment person for an off premises caterer. See if you'd really like it.
> Don't just sit there on the sidelines wondering your whole life.

Interesting. Very, very clear comment.

Let's do this. 1-800-FLOWERS.com is something that I'm a customer of. I love when an event comes around and I need your services. And some of what's so critical, so important, such a bedrock of your success is the power of you creating relationships. Not just with you and your employees, but with all of you and your customers. I have business owners and entrepreneurs listening right now. What are some tips or strategies or techniques that they can use? Can you talk a moment about the power of relationships? The power of what you call *the contact economy?*

People kid me about the fact that my first career was in social work. How could that possibly be relevant to running 1-800-FLOWERS.com today? My point is that I think that they are amazingly similar, Mike. Because the skills, the personality, the characteristics that I learned to develop from those 10 young men I worked with in that group all those many years ago are the same skills that I use today. That was my job then, was to develop a relationship.

I couldn't have a relationship with the group. That was the first mistake I made. I needed to develop relationships with individuals because developing contacts where you break through and you have a personal contact with an individual is the first step toward developing a relationship. And everything becomes a basis of a relationship. We're fortunate enough to live in an economic time right now that is fabulous. It the best we've ever seen. So there are plenty of opportunities.

What's our favorite restaurant on Long Island? What's our favorite restaurant in any town we live in? It's the restaurant that knows our name. James Beard said that many years ago. *The key to a great restaurant and your recommendations is the one that knows your name.* Especially the communities that we live in. They are fairly impersonal. There isn't a sense of neighborhood that we ultimately like to see in every town. In some there are but in some there aren't.

We all gravitate. Where do we go to get our haircut? It's where we've developed a feeling of comfort. Where we know the people. Where we're recognized. Where they know that we are Yankee fans, or Met fans, so we'll talk about that.

197

Our job as florists, too, is to develop relationships. Some of our customers will never ever come into one of our stores, and at 1-800-FLOWERS.com you know that you can come *to* our store either literally through our front door or *virtually* by way of the telephone or by way of the Internet.

So our job is to develop a relationship with a customer and a lot of people know about us because of our use of technology. But if there's something we're *not*, it's a high tech company.

What we *are* is a high touch company.

(To listeners)

You're ready to jump out of your chair and visit one of the most famous websites ever invented. 1-800-FLOWERS.com, for all your needs.

Stop and Sell the Roses - Lessons for Business and Life. You need to run after the show to your local bookstore and say, "I want *Stop and Sell the Roses*!"

(Back to Jim)

What I am going to do right now, Jim, I'm going to put on my famous two-minute warning. What that means is we're going to keep the answers as concise as possible. Get as much out as we can and rock 'n roll. Sound good?

Sounds good to me.

Ok.

Something that interests me, and you mentioned it in your material in your book, is the *power*, the *importance*, the *effectiveness* of using praise. Can you talk about your experience with praise, so listeners can use it to create a better, more satisfying relationship with their employees?

I grew up working for a dad who was a tough task master. I also worked for another fellow whose clothing store I worked in for many years through high school and

198

college. And neither of them would have much in terms of praise.

In fact, we employees had to go out of our way to find ways of keeping score ourselves.

If you want to have a good working environment, if you want to let people know that they're appreciated, I think the first rule is *if they are doing a good job, tell them.*

It's as basic and elementary as can be. But nothing makes me feel better than hearing a few times, "hey, you did a good job."

It doesn't mean that you have to be their boss, you can tell someone working with you, for you, I just think *when you see it, say it.*

Very simple, very clear.

I believe after the last count, 10%, if I'm correct, of your business is done through the Internet or a huge amount is. The Internet is a very challenging media these days and you have been so successful. What tips, a couple of things, a couple of keys that business owners listening can grab from your positive experience and use in their own business?

I can't think, Mike, of a *business* out there that should not be involved in the Internet! I can't think of the *individual* who shouldn't be playing and experimenting and learning about the Internet. In 1970 they invented the silicon chip and created the information revolution, which has absolutely radically *altered* the landscape in terms of the economy and economies in the world today. And the next big turbo charge to that revolution was the democratization of the Internet. It's having a huge impact. I don't care if you're the wine merchant, liquor store, or you're the drycleaner, or you're the florist. You need to *understand* the Internet and play with it. How it can impact your customers. How it can change your business life. Because if *you* don't know it, your *competition* will. And they'll change your life very radically.

(To listeners)

You need to get your hands on *Stop and Sell the Roses*. I'm telling you. I'm holding it right now right in front of me. I'm absolutely honored. You need to read this book. Go run down to a local book store when we're done here.

(Back to Jim)

Jim, your famous 10 semi-commandments, really 11. I want to just touch on one or two of them very briefly. Something very interesting is number 9. This is interesting. It says, "high margins aren't always important." Can you walk us through with the power of that principal?

Simple.

High margins attract a lot of talent. Any business that has ridiculously high margins is going to attract ridiculous competition. Very talented competition that eventually will knock down the margins. So, the difference will have to come out of your product and service.

So, unless you happen to be the smartest person in the world, and you may have that person in your audience, *don't try to outsmart the smartest.*

Figure out a business that you're interested in. Figure out an opportunity that gets you excited. Figure out a point that you can get started, don't worry about the margins. If there are other businesses out there that are successful, you can be successful, too. But you can bring new technology and techniques. You can find ways of trimming your expenses to give you the competitive advantage even in a low margin business.

Interesting.

Let's get to another commandment or two. *The power of branding yourself.*

I get the opportunity to speak to audiences pretty regularly around the country. And I'll ask people often, "how many people in the audience are *brand managers*?" I ask for a show of hands and I'll get six or 12 hands that go up in a room of about 1,000 people. They'll tell us, "yes, they're brand managers."

My comment is that they are wrong. Every single one of them is a brand manager. Mike Litman is *clearly* a brand manager. He is managing not only the brand of his program, but the brand of himself. Each of us is a brand manager.

What I define as a brand is this. If I took six people, three associates of yours from the broadcast world and three friends of yours, locked them in a room, tied each one of them to a chair and injected them with a truth potion and said, "tell me about Mike Litman." The first three or four sentences would be *your* brand definition *in their eyes*.

Whether you're an employee or you're looking at a community situation or you are looking at a business situation, everything that you say and/or *do* impacts people's perception of you. Which is your brand.

Interesting. Let's talk here.

Many people know you. They see you on television in your 1-800-FLOWERS.com ads. Can you tell us a little bit, from an advertising perspective, why you decided to make that job into *you* being the brand?

It was many years ago and back then we weren't as well known a brand. 1-800-FLOWERS.com was clearly not as well known.

We're a family business who operates florists, which is a very personal business, and there were a few company names.

We were the first company whose name was a telephone number. We were the first company whose name was a telephone number who used that *same* name to become a brand and used it, of course, in *several* different channels, *not* just the telephone. Our *stores* are called 1-800-FLOWERS.com, and our *website* is called 1-800-FLOWERS.com.

But it was impersonal and our agency made a recommendation for several years that we personalize it by putting someone who is clearly "nutty passionate" about

201

flowers, and what they can do for people's lives, and for me to step in front.

For years we resisted it. And several years ago when we decided to try it, it was a big success because it personalized our brand to show that we are real people. A real family of McCanns who are nuts about what we do as florists.

(To listeners)

We've got about a minute left before we wrap up here with the one, the only Jim McCann. *Stop and Sell the Roses* is a must read. If you ever had an inkling of a thought of being in business, you are in business, and even if you are just listening right now, and not in business, it's just a touching human story of an individual who in a span of his life went from a social worker to a florist to a mega entrepreneur. Entrepreneur of the year. Retailer of the year. Direct marketer of the year. The guy is just absolutely fabulous.

(Back to Jim)

Are there any books through your transformation that have impacted you that you can recommend? Anything that you came across in your life that you can recommend to my listeners right now?

Michael, I'm a ferocious reader. I read everything I can, whether it's periodicals or books. I don't get to read as many books as I'd like. But, there is a book by Michael Tracy that I recommend called *The Discipline of Market Leaders,* which I think lays out in blueprint form how you have to think about your product or service and how you market it in a way so you put your energies into resources.

Great. Jim, unfortunately, this is the part of the show that I never want to happen, but it always does. It's been an absolutely tremendous, fast-paced and profitable time, Jim. I look forward to seeing you again. Jim McCann, thank you for appearing on *The Mike Litman Show.*

203

204

Chapter Nine

Conversation with Jay Conrad Levinson

(Introduction to the listeners)

Tonight is an absolutely explosive show! The ingredients, the recipe tonight will blow your mind. We're going hard-core tonight. Why? Listen to this...

Seventeen years ago a revolution in the business world took place. At that point we didn't know about it. What happened is this: a book was published. A revolution transformed the world of business.

The book's been published in 37 languages. The author is here live tonight. The book, *Guerrilla Marketing*. The author, the great Jay Conrad Levinson.

Tonight we talk about Guerrilla Marketing. We talk about the distinction between guerrilla marketing and traditional marketing. We talk about the characteristics. How *you* can become a guerrilla and guerrilla-size your business by taking it to the next level. We'll talk about using this stuff online.

Jay Conrad Levinson, the one and only author of the best-selling marketing series ever is on the line.

His books are now the basis of many MBA courses around the country.

The Marlboro Man commercials. Fly the Friendly Skies of United Airlines. Pillsbury Doughboy. This is one of the integral, important guys behind 3 of the greatest advertising campaigns in this century.

Jay Conrad Levinson, my dime, your dance floor. Welcome to *The Mike Litman Show.*

Mike, it is really good to be here. You've got me psyched. I'm excited to be talking to your listeners and to you.

Thank you very much. There's people all around the world excited tonight to learn the information. They've read the books *Guerrilla Marketing* and all outlets from there.

Before we get into a little bit about how this all started, Jay, about how this all started. I want to lay a foundation here. I want to lay a core here. Walk my audience through the difference between guerrilla marketing and what we call traditional marketing.

Well, I used to compare guerrilla marketing with text book marketing. But I can't do that anymore now that *Guerrilla Marketing* is the text book in so many universities.

So, I compare it with traditional marketing and there are 19 differences.

People who really care about marketing and getting profits for their business will get a paper and a pencil and start writing down these differences. Because these are not only the differences between guerrilla marketing and traditional marketing, but they are the way of marketing around the world. The way of the world these days cause marketing is being transformed like crazy.

The first difference is traditional marketing says, if you want to market your business, you've got to invest money. *Guerrilla Marketing* says, hey, if you want to invest money, you can, but you don't really have to. Your primary investments should be time, energy, and imagination.

Jay, say that line again.

Your primary investments should be time, energy and imagination. If you're willing to invest those, you won't have to invest as much money.

A second difference is that traditional marketing intimidates too many people.

It scares them.

They're not really sure what marketing is.

It's enshrouded by a mystique, and so they just don't do it rather than dare make a mistake.

They're not sure if marketing includes advertising or if it includes the Internet, or if it includes selling.

So, with *Guerrilla Marketing,* the difference is that *Guerrilla Marketing* totally removes the mystique from the marketing process.

There is absolutely nothing about it that is smoky or hazy or scary and by the time this hour is over, anybody listening will notice that there is no more mystique around marketing.

The third difference is that, well, I should start from the beginning…

I was teaching a course at the University of California in Berkeley. The extension division. It was about running your own business, and people asked if I could recommend a book on marketing for people with a limited budget. I said I'd give it a shot.

I went to the library at Berkeley, but there were no books written for people with small budgets. I went to the library at Stanford. I went to the City of San Francisco and Los Angeles. None of those libraries had books for people with limited budgets.

All the books they had on marketing were written for people who could spend $30,000 a month, which was not my students.

So, as a service to my students, I wrote *Guerrilla Marketing* not knowing it would take on a life of its own.

So, every word on every line on every page of every *Guerrilla Marketing* book is geared to small business.

That makes it very different than traditional marketing, which has always been geared to big business.

A fourth difference is that traditional marketing is always based its performance on how many sales it makes, how much traffic comes through the door, or how many responses they get to an offer.

207

> *Guerrilla Marketing* says those are the wrong answers. Those are the wrong numbers to be looking at. The only number that matters are your *profits*. Anybody can have high sales.

Say that again. We're focusing on this word "profits" instead of sales. Walk us through that.

> Because it's very easy for anybody to enjoy high sales. But it's hard to make money on each one of those sales.
>
> Some people spend $50 to make a sale on something where their profit is $40. So, they are *losing* $10 each time they make a sale.
>
> *Guerrillas* only look at that number "profits". And everything they do is oriented to increasing the beauty of their of bottom line.
>
> They don't care as much about sales as they do about profits. The only thing that matters is how much is left over *after* the expenses have been paid.
>
> A fifth difference is that traditional marketing has always been based on experience and judgment, which is a fancy way of saying guesswork.
>
> People who are guerrilla marketers know they can't afford the wrong guesses and don't want to make them.
>
> So *Guerrilla Marketing* is based as much as possible upon *psychology*. Actual laws of human behavior.
>
> For example, we know that 90% of all purchase decisions are made in the unconscious mind and they also now know a slam dunk manner of accessing the unconscious mind.

Tell me about that, Jay. Tell us about that one.

> The way to do that is through repetition.
>
> Purchase decisions are made in the unconscious mind, which is 90% of our brain.
>
> How do you access that unconscious mind? Through *repetition*.

The more people hear it, the more it gets through to that unconscious where the purchase decision is made.

Guerrilla marketing *leans* on psychology as much as possible.

The sixth difference is - and there are 19 differences - traditional marketing says grow your business and *then* start diversifying.

Guerrilla marketing says forget that thought.

Grow your business if you want, but make sure you maintain your focus. Don't think of diversification, think of maintaining your focus.

That's pretty darn hard.

The seventh one is one of the most important differences.

Traditional marketing has always said the way to grow a business is linearly, which is to say by adding new customers on a regular basis. Now that's a very expensive way to grow.

Guerrilla marketing says the way to grow your company is *geometrically*.

What that means is to *enlarge the size of each transaction* that you make. Have *more transactions* per year with *each* one of your customers. And then tap the enormous *referral* power of those customers. Because they all have friends. Associates who might also become customers and at the same time, add even *more* new customers by referring others themselves.

Let me jump right in here.

What you're saying right here I don't want to wash over because you're laying out three different million dollar techniques.

Can you talk to the small business owner listening right now?

Can you go through a little bit deeper in that ability to grow geometrically, Jay?

Talk about an example, if you can, about how do you increase the frequency? How do you increase the size of the order? How do they grow geometrically? Can you walk us through that a bit?

I sure can. That's a great question.

The first part of growing geometrically is to enlarge the size of each transaction. That is realizing that once a person has decided to buy from you, it's not going to cost you anything to upgrade the size of their order.

If they want to buy what ever it is that you are selling, you should have a deluxe version, or package version so that the *size* of that transaction is larger than it normally would be.

So you are saying give them the *option* of spending more money if they want to.

Yes.

Have something for them to spend it on. Most people don't have an upgraded or a deluxe version.

I'm saying, get one.

Bookstores, for example. Some bookstores sell books, book by book. Other bookstores put the books into gift baskets and have maybe four or five related books in one basket. So, when a person goes to that bookstore they appreciate the book seller's recommendation of those five books. Then that transaction is larger.

By keeping track of what your customers like, whatever it is, you can then stay in touch with them so that they will make more transactions with you during the course of the year.

By staying in touch with them through your follow up they are going make more transactions.

Then, of course, all of your customers are members of a business, or go to a school, or are members of a church, or a members of a club, or have a lot of friends. They have a network and they can talk to these people and this is free marketing for you. They have enormous ability to give you referrals, all you've got to do is ask.

If you are taking care of your customers by staying in touch with them, when you ask them for the names of three people who might benefit from hearing from you, or getting on your mailing list, and you give them a post-paid envelope or you do it online and make it very simple for them, they're going to do it. They want you to succeed. They know you take good care of your customers. You're only asking for three names. So they'll be happy to do that.

At the same time, do the regular marketing that you'll hear about as we go on, and then you're growing geometrically. You're growing four different directions. You're enlarging each transaction. You are having more transactions per year. You're tapping that referral power of each customer so that you can start having transactions with those people too and you're bringing in other members of the universe through the other marketing that you're doing.

If you are growing in four directions at once, It's pretty hard to go out of business. It's pretty hard to lose money.

Your cost of marketing goes down and your profits go up because it costs you 1/6 as much to sell something to an existing customer than to sell to somebody brand new.

That's what I'm going to call Four Directions to Absolute Fortune! The four things that you just laid out, Jay.

What I want to do is hit rewind before we go forward. You talked about follow up. You talked about the ability to get back in front of that customer for a few different reasons.

To the small businessman or woman listening right now, online, offline, is there any weapons in your arsenal that you can recommend to make that follow up efficient, effective and worthwhile for that business owner?

I sure do and that's the eighth difference between traditional and guerrilla marketing.

It's a shocking fact. 70% of business that is lost in America is lost due to apathy after the sale. It's lost due to customers being ignored after they've made the purchase.

Business isn't lost due to bad quality or poor service. It's lost due to customers being ignored.

So, guerrillas never ignore a customer. That's one of the big differences. They are very big on follow up.

211

Let me give you an example of what I am talking about with some real numbers.

Let's say a person has got a business.

Whenever they sell a product they earn $100 profit.

Let's say they don't have a clue about follow up or guerrilla marketing.

So that means when a person buys what they sell, they make a hundred dollar profit. They put it into their pocket and that person leaves.

So that means that one person represented $100 to their lives.

But let's say now that you get another person who understands follow up. The purpose of it and the point of it. They understands guerrilla marketing.

Here's what that means: it means that that person will send out thank you notes to the person who made the purchase within 48 hours.

How many times in your life have you made a purchase and received a thank you note within 48 hours? Probably once, or maybe never.

So understand that. Then at the end of 30 days you send them a note. Just a letter where you ask if they are happy with the purchase they made and do they have any questions.

Notice you are not trying to sell them anything. You're just trying to make sure they are happy with what they have and that they are not confused about it.

At the end of three months, you get in touch with them again. This time maybe by telephone call. Maybe with email. Or, maybe with a letter. Here you are making them a special offer that is a product or service that's connected with their original purchase.

They are going to be inclined to pay attention to you because they know that you stayed in touch with them. You've shown that you're not just out to get their money, but that you to make sure they are happy.

At the end of six months, they get a customer questionnaire from you. You ask questions about them with a little paragraph at the top, and you say, "Sorry to be asking so many questions, but the more we know about you the better service we can be to you."

You maybe ask them questions, like what sports team do they root for, what kind of car do the drive, what kind of job do they have, what kind of interests do their kids have? You ask a lot of personal questions.

They don't mind giving you that information, cause it makes sense to them. It's true. The more you know about them, the better you can service them.

So that's part of follow up is learning about them.

Maybe at the end of nine months you might send them a note congratulating them of their daughter making the cheerleading squad. They get an anniversary card from you one year after having been your customer congratulating them on their anniversary of them being a customer.

As a result of staying in touch with them on a regular basis like this, and it doesn't end at the course of the year, one person will end up making *three* purchases from you.

They will end up making the purchase and they will end up recommending your business to four people during the course of the year. Even over and above the ones that you asked for.

Now, their relationship with you will last not one trans-action as so often happens, but it will last as long as 20 years.

If you do the math on that, it means that one customer is worth $200,000 to you if you understand follow up.

It doesn't cost much money to do that at all.

But understand follow up. The thank you notes. The note making sure that they are happy. Stay in touch with them by phone, email, fax, in person, or with letters, whatever it takes. Stay in touch with them and make them realize that you know them and connect with them as a human being not just as a customer.

Once they get that from you, it's going to get easy for them to recommend your business to other people.

The ninth difference between guerrilla marketing and traditional marketing is that traditional marketing has always said scan the horizon to see which competitors you can obliterate.

One of my things says that's just nonsense. Don't think like that. Instead scan the horizon for those businesses with which you might cooperate.

Say that again.

Don't look around for businesses that are competitors that you can obliterate, instead look around for other businesses that have the same kind of prospects and the same kind of standard that you do and look for companies with which you can cooperate.

You watch television. You see a commercial. You think it's from McDonalds. Midway through you think it's from Coca-Cola. By the time it's over it was for The Lion King or Pocahontas.

There's lots of that we call fusion marketing.

There's lots of that going on the world today. Especially on small business levels because if you do that fusion marketing, connecting up with other businesses, with the idea of forming a joint marketing venture just for a short time, you'll find you can reach more people.

If your reach goes up, the cost goes down because you are sharing it with other people.

In Japan, for example, seven, eight, nine businesses get together in fusion marketing campaigns.

They are able to advertise and market all over the place and it costs them just a fraction because so many people are in on it.

In the Unites States, more and more small businesses are learning to do that same thing. To wrap their mind around the idea of *cooperation* more than competition.

Let me jump in right now. Because after this show you and I are going to invoice my listeners about $20 to $25,000.

(To the listeners)

If you're listening right now, what I have to tell you and hopefully you pick up, is Jay Conrad Levinson, best-selling author, just laid out for you a free marketing plan.

Did you here that?

From day one to the 12th month. With the notes, with the anniversaries, with the surveys. That is absolutely priceless information!

(Back to Jay)

Jay, we've gone through about nine differences and maybe we get to a few more as we proceed.

I love on this show to talk about the mind set. To talk about the personality traits. To talk about what someone needs inside to produce these results outside.

What kind of traits or characteristics does a successful guerrilla marketer have?

Well, I'll tell you Mike. I've been noticing the personalities of the people who run successful marketing campaigns in the United States, in Europe, and in the Far East. I've noticed the personality traits of people at the helm of Fortune 500 companies and the personality traits of people who are in small start-ups who want to be like the Fortune 500 companies.

The people in charge of the marketing for successful companies seem to have the same personality traits.

I keep looking for differences. Looking for a person with a different kind of personality. But, I can't find any differences.

The personalities of the people who are running really successful profit-producing marketing for all sized companies have 12 personality traits in common.

The first one, which may be the most important one, is based on a study that was taken in the United States.

It amazes me that they would even attempt to answer this question.

215

Here's what the question was: How many times must your marketing message penetrate a person's mind to move them from the state that we call total apathy, which means they've never heard of you, to the state of purchase readiness which means they want to buy like crazy what you are selling?

That's a hard question. How many times must your message penetrate a person's mind?

Amazingly, the researchers came up with an answer.

The answer they came up with was nine.

Your message has to penetrate a person's mind nine times to move them from a state of total apathy, that means they've never heard of you, to purchase readiness, which means boy, they are ready to buy right now.

Okay, that's the good news.

Here's the bad news. For every three times you put out the word, people aren't paying attention two times.

They have more important things to do in their lives than pay attention to your marketing.

So, you've got to put the word out three times to penetrate the mind one time. And what happens when that happens? Nothing happens, absolutely nothing.

So now you put the word out six times.

Now you've penetrated their minds two times.

Now, something happens.

They realize they've heard of you before.

But, that's as far as it goes. You put the word out six times but all they've done is realize that they have heard of you.

Now you put the word out nine times and you've penetrated their minds three times.

This is when they think, 'hey, I've seen that persons marketing before' and unconsciously they think, 'people who continue marketing must be successful companies.' But, that's all they think, and nothing else happens.

Now you put the word out 12 times, and you've penetrated their minds four times. This is when they start to look around to see if they can find your name in other places.

216

They are not even going to read your ad yet or pay attention to your direct mail letter. But they are going to look around to see if there are other signs of you.

Now, you put the word out 15 times. So, you've penetrated their minds five times.

This is the time that they are going to read every word of your ad, or brochure, and this is when they are going to call and ask for your brochure.

If you have a website, this is the time they are going to go online and click over to your website and really check it out.

Notice they are not nearly ready to buy. But the whole idea of selling something is a matter of creating momentum and you've created the right momentum.

Now, here's what happens in real life - I hate it, but this is what happens - people do the right thing with the right marketing plan, the right words, the right everything, and at the end of 15 times of putting out the word, they assume, 'God if the world is not beating a path to my door, I must be doing everything wrong.' So, they abandon their marketing campaign.

They use different media. They have a different message. They come up with different graphics. Different headlines. Different everything and it's the worst thing for them to do.

It's like starting back at square one. You've got to hang in there.

Put the word out 18 times. Then you've penetrated a person's mind six times, and this is when they think that maybe they should rethink you seriously. When might they make the purchase from you?

Then put the word out 21 times. You'll have penetrated their minds seven times, and this is when they actually think to themselves, 'where am I going to get the money?' This is where they think very seriously to themselves, 'when will I do it? When will I get the money?' They are that close to purchasing.

Now you put the word out 24 times. You've penetrated their mind eight times. This is when they check with whoever

217

it is that they have to check with before making the purchase. Their boss, or their partner, or their wife or their husband. Whoever it is that they have to check with, this is the phase they'll do it.

Now you put the word out 27 times. You've penetrated their mind nine times. Now they buy what you're selling and they listen to what you are saying.

If you want to enlarge the size of the transaction now you've earned that trust over this period of time.

So, the first personality trait of successful guerrillas, obviously, is *patience*.

Who else could hang in there that long through the whole process to take place, but someone with patience? Because marketing is not an event, it's a *process*.

Say that again, Jay.

Marketing is not an event, it's a process.
It takes a lot of patience to hang in there for that whole process to happen.

Most people think marketing is something you do. Put the word out online. Send a letter or post card. Or, put a yellow pages ad in and I'm going to sell. No way. It doesn't work like that.

You need the patience to hang in there. We talked about repetition before.

The second personality characteristic is imagination.

By that I don't mean dreaming up headlines or copy.

Instead, by imagination, I mean that if you are going to do a mailing, face up to the fact that people are assaulted with a blizzard of direct mail. They are going to toss most of it away.

So, decide that if you are going to do a mailing, if you really want to break through the clutter, decide to invest in first class postage. Which means 34¢.

But don't buy a 34¢ stamp. Because anybody can do that.

Instead by 11 stamps. Then on each letter put a 6¢ stamp, two 4¢ stamps, four 3¢ stamps, and four 2¢ stamps and it adds up to 34¢.

Then when the person gets the letter, for the first time in their life they see a letter with 11 stamps on it.

They are definitely going to open that letter.

That's a million dollar technique right there.

Right. That breaks through the clutter.

That gets you a response rate.

When you hear about direct mail, when you study direct mail, you learn that a healthy response rate is 2%.

Doing things like this, your response rates are 10 and 20% or higher.

All it takes, as I said, is imagination.

The third personality characteristic after patience and imagination, is *sensitivity*.

Successful guerrillas are sensitive to the market, to this particular time in history, and to the place in which they are marketing. Urban is different than rural. They are sensitive to the competition, what the competition is saying, etc.

Mainly they are sensitive to what's on their prospect's mind right now. What are their prospects thinking right now. That's what they are really sensitive to.

The fourth personality characteristic is ego strength.

Here is what I mean by ego strength: You launch a marketing campaign and you are saying the right words in the right places to the right people. Guess who are the first people to get bored with your marketing?

The answer is your coworkers. Your employees. Your family.

They are the people who are going to say, "hey I'm getting a little tired of the marketing you are doing, why don't you change it."

So, you need an ego to stand up to these people, to give them a nice warm hug and then send them on their way knowing they don't know beans about marketing.

The people who love you the most, give you the worst marketing advise.

You need the ego to stand up to those people and realize that the people who have only heard your message four times are certainly not bored.

The people who have already purchased from you will never be bored. They'll spend the rest of their lives paying attention to your marketing to justify the fact that they do business with you.

The fifth personality characteristic, after patience and imagination, and after sensitivity and ego strength is *aggressiveness*.

You've got to be aggressive.

There are a hundred different weapons in guerrilla marketing. By the way, 62 of those weapons are free, and the whole list of 100 marketing weapons we have published on the website at gmarketingcoach.com

I saw that list today, it's mind blowing.

It's impossible right now to go through the 100 weapons. But at gmarketingcoach.com it's easy.

So guerrillas are aggressive in that they know there's 100 marketing weapons they can use and 62 of them are free. So, they are aggressive in how many weapons they use.

They are also aggressive in how much they invest in the marketing process. In the year 2000 the average US business only invested 4% of their gross sales in marketing. Four percent. So, the guerrilla thinks 4%? Is that all?

Well, the average business doesn't do very well. What would happen if I invested 8%? So, aggressiveness is one of the trademarks in a guerrilla.

A sixth personality characteristic is that guerrillas embrace *change*.

They're not scared of change.

They don't ignore change. They don't pray that change will go away. They open their minds to change and they embrace it.

They don't embrace change just to change, but to improve.

A lot of things that are happening in the world today are improvements over the way business used to be done.

A seventh personality characteristic is that unlike other people, guerrillas are very generous.

Instead of thinking of what they could be taking from their customers, they think, "what can I *give* to my customer?"

They know what marketing really is.

What marketing really is, is an opportunity for them to help their customers succeed in whatever it is their customers want to succeed in.

Maybe it's making more money. Maybe it's attracting a mate. Maybe it's losing weight.

Whatever it is that their customers want to do, they give information to help that person do that.

They think, 'what can I give away?

They give it away on their website. They give it in free consultations. They give it away in free demonstrations. They give it away in the form of free gifts.

They think of what they can give. Then the more they think that thought, the more they get. Because people know the difference between a generous person and a grabby, picky person.

Guerrillas are very generous.

Another thing they are, Mike, which is what you are too, number eight is they are energetic people.

They know that you cannot conquer foes, win battles, market aggressively unless you put forth the energy.

Knowing it is not enough. You've got to really have the energy to do it to get excited about it. To be excited about the opportunities to do things in marketing that your competitor's have never dreamt about.

Unless you have that energy, all your information goes for naught.

The ninth personality characteristic has a lot to do with seagulls.

Picture a seagull. Seagulls fly in circles in the sky. Ever increasing circles. Constant circles in the sky. That's all they do is fly in circles and eventually they land because they see food and they eat their fill and then they go right back up in the sky and they fly in circles again.

They just can't help it. Their strongest instinct is to fly in circles looking for food.

Well guerrillas have one instinct that is just as strong. It's the strongest instinct in the mind of a guerrilla. It's the need for constant *learning*.

Say that again.

The strongest instinct in the mind of the guerrilla marketer, the guerrilla business person, or the guerrilla entrepreneur is the idea of constant learning.

So, self-education is a real key in making this process work over time?

Self education is *the* key, Mike. Because life is no longer a matter of learning everything there is about a topic.

Instead, life is a matter of learning one thing after another and the only way to do that is by doing it yourself.

Only you are in charge of doing that.

School can help you. But, *you* are the only person who can do the constant learning. Because it doesn't just last four years. It lasts for the rest of your life.

So, you have to have a passion and desire to do that constant learning.

Get excited. Because the Internet makes it so available to you right now.

Before we get to that, let me jump in right here, Jay.

What you're talking about Jay as I'm just sitting here listening, is absolutely amazing.

I want to rewind back to personality trait number one.

You talked about patience. The ability to stay with the message.

Now, there is someone listening right now and we're talking about 15 times, 18 times, going on and getting out there.

How do I know if my message is wrong? Is there a way to test?

When do I know maybe it's not the repetition I need, but maybe I need a new message?

Is there anything that I can view and look for to give me an eye-opening experience, that maybe, 'hey, this isn't going to work'?

Yes.

It depends a lot on the kind of product.

For example, just to use real facts, one of the hardest things to get a person to do is to change cigarette brands.

Because those who smoke cigarettes are very connected to the brand they are smoking.

Then there is a product that has the least brand loyalty. It's with shampoos.

Most women buy four different kinds of shampoos in the course of the year.

It's very easy to switch their loyalty when it comes to shampoos.

So, it depends on the product.

I tell my clients that if they do everything right, at the end of three months they're still going to see absolutely no sign that their marketing is working.

They have to hang in there and at the end of six months, they're going to begin to see the first glimmers that it is working.

Not just because business is up, but because people will mention that they have seen the marketing.

At the end of nine months, they will realize that it is going up every month now.

At the end of a year they are certain that it works because every month is better than the month before.

So, it's P & P. It's patience and persistence to your message and your marketing?

Get Two Valuable FREE Gifts At: www.cwmbook.com

Absolutely, and no matter how good your message is, if you don't have that patience it's not going to hit home.

The graveyards of marketing are littered with wonderful campaigns that were just abandoned because they didn't work in a hurry.

But great ones don't work in a hurry.

So the guerrilla marketing mindset, to win and to succeed at guerrilla marketing, is first an inner resolve before we even start an outer action. Is that right.

That's exactly right.

The inner resolve is what makes it happen.

In the story I'm about to tell you'll hear how that inner resolve is what made the most successfully marketed brand in history a success.

I just want to go through the last three personality traits of guerrillas first.

So, number 10 is, guerrillas like people.

They're all people persons.

They all enjoy being with people.

They know that it's people who help *make* what they are selling, *sell* what their selling, and who *buy* what they are selling.

The 11th personality characteristic is that guerrillas are able to maintain their focus.

They don't get easily distracted.

The final, the 12th one. First we said patience. Then imagination, sensitivity, ego strength, aggressiveness, embracing change, generosity, energetic, constant learning, being a people person, maintaining focus.

The 12th, which I think is about as important as the first, is that guerrillas take *action*.

They *do* things. They don't talk about it or think about it. They actually *take action* on what they learn.

Most people are great at absorbing information. They listen to the radio, they go on line, they read books, they listen to tapes, and they absorb a lot of information. But,

224

only a small percentage of those people take action on what they've learned.

If you didn't take action 17 years ago, we would never have the Guerrilla Marketing series.

That's exactly the truth. That's why I did it. That's why we have that site gmarketingcoach.com to help people take action.

I'm on the phone with them live once a week because we know that some people want to take action in their hearts, but they're just not able to get it together to do that.

So, taking action is the 12th personality characteristic.

Jay, you mention that most people haven't yet been able to do the taking action part.

What I've noticed is that: Jay Conrad Levinson, Mark Joyner, Robert Allen...there's a thread that makes the difference of why we are buying their stuff. It's that these people have all taken action.

It's almost like, Jay, tell me if you concur here, once you start doing something, once you start getting out there, getting your message out there, wonderful things happen. But, it won't happen if you're not doing anything.

How do you get off the couch, how do you start going? Any tips you can share with people?

Yes.

Here's the way I do it, and this really works...

I just keep a regular date book, the kind that you write by hand in. Not an electronic thing, as much as I love computers. I have just a regular date book and I *write down* what I am going to do.

I work a three-day week.

I've been working, from my home, a three-day week since 1971.

I feel anybody can do it. That's mainly why I started writing books is to let people know that they can do it too.

What I do is, I write the tasks to do on the days I'm going to do them.

So, I write my tasks on a Monday, Tuesday and Wednesday, those are the days that I work.

Today, I was out hiking all day. Now I'm back hanging out and talking to you and I don't consider this work, to be talking with you Mike.

So, I write those tasks on those days. Then if I see that I am writing those tasks and it's filling up the day, I stop and I move it over to another day.

When I've got the Mondays, the Tuesdays and the Wednesdays filled up, I flip the pages until I get to the next Monday and then write those tasks in there.

When I'm writing those tasks, I know those are promises I'm making to myself.

I'm not going to write it down unless I realize that it's a promise that I am making to myself, and guerrillas keep their promises. Especially the promises that they make to themselves. They keep their promises to everybody.

But, in order to take action, you've got to put it in *writing*.

Say that again.

One of the more important things I'll be saying is that *in order to really put things into action, you've got to first put them into writing.*

Once you've put them into writing, the power of the written word will enable you to focus on what you are supposed to do and then do it.

If you've written it down on a specific day to do it, then you can do it on that day.

It's a promise you're making to yourself.

If you can't keep the promises you are making to yourself, you may as well think about going into another line of work, or get a job, a regular 9 to 5 job.

But, I'm talking about going way beyond that and living a whole kind of better life. I'm not talking about getting rich quick. I'm talking about just balancing your life and these are ways to do it.

I'll give you the single most important word and this is the single most important word that I'm going to say.

You've already talked about it, Mike. This is part of what makes you happen.

If you had to go through the one single secret of guerrilla marketing or of all marketing, there is a one word answer to this. It's the main secret of marketing and guerrilla marketing.

The answer begins with a flashback to something that happened in my life, in my own career.

I was working for a large advertising agency in Chicago. We were called into a cigarette company in New York because they had a brand that was in 31st place. It was perceived as a feminine brand and, although in those days it was true that more women smoked than men, men smoked more cigarettes.

They wanted to know if we could change the perception of the brand around so that it was more masculine and if we could do something about being ranked 31st.

So, we said we'd give it a shot.

We sent a couple of photographers and an art director to a friend's ranch in West Texas. Then we told him to spend two weeks shooting photographs of what cowboys do on a real ranch.

We said, "don't take those posed pictures.

Don't let them know what you are doing.

Don't have any cows in the pictures. Horses and cowboys. No women, just men.

Just take pictures for two weeks."

While they were doing that, we came up with a fictional place and we called it Marlboro Country.

Then we came up with a theme line.

The theme line was, "Come to where the flavor is. Come to Marlboro Country."

So, the photographers came back.

We developed the pictures and we blew them up.

Then we pasted these words on the pictures. It was like 'here are cowboys doing what cowboys really do' and it said,

227

"Come to where the flavor is. Come to Marlboro Country" with a picture of the package.

We thought, 'this is really cool. This was what we needed.'

So, we go to O'Hare. We fly to JFK and we tell the taxi driver we want to go to number two Park Avenue, which is where Phillip Morris is located - that's the parent company of Marlboro, and we go up there and we present the Marlboro campaign to the Marlboro brand group.

They were blown away.

They liked it so much, that they agreed to invest $18 million in it the first year.

It's a lot of money now and it was a lot of money then.

In those days, it was illegal promote carcinogens on radio and television. So, we rented the music to the Magnificent Seven for our television commercials.

The Marlboro Man became a cultural icon.

At the end of the year he was all over the place: radio, television, magazines, newspapers, billboards.

Of course we went back to New York to get our high fives and pats on the back. But, we found out that after a year and $18 million, the brand that had been the 31st largest selling cigarette in the country was still the 31st largest selling cigarette in the country.

Worse than that, focus group interviews in 10 cities around the United States showed us that this brand was still perceived as a feminine brand.

Now here we've been showing these macho cowboys doing what cowboys really do on a real ranch. Yet still the brand was perceived of as feminine.

So now, we flash to today and we see that Marlboros are the number one selling cigarette in America.

It's number one to men. It's number one to women.

It's the number one selling cigarette in the world.

In fact, one out of every five cigarettes sold in the world is a Marlboro.

So, here's the shocker: absolutely nothing about the marketing has changed. Nothing.

It's still Marlboro. It's still Marlboro Country. It's still cowboys. It's still, "Come to where the flavor is."

It's exactly the same as it was in the first reel we did. No more radio. No more television. But, it's a lot of the same art designs that we used. A lot of the same graphics. A lot of the same models, except for those poor guys who died of lung cancer.

So, that brings us back to the one-word answer as to what makes marketing work, and the answer, obviously, is "commitment."

Say that again.

I said, "there's a one-word answer to what makes marketing work and the answer to that is *commitment*."

What makes a marriage work? Commitment.

What makes a business work? Commitment.

What makes your garden grow? Commitment.

Your commitment to a marketing plan is going to make your marketing work.

I don't like admitting this in public, but I'll say it: mediocre marketing *with* commitment works a lot better than brilliant marketing *without* commitment.

So, the name of the game really and truly with marketing is *get a plan*, very simple plan. Seven sentences long. That's all it has to be. Then *commit* to that plan.

Really I recommend you test first the things you're going to do in small markets. In newspapers or mailings. So that you don't commit to the wrong kind of thing.

Get a feeling by testing and experimenting. Then commit to that, and don't expect miracles, because marketing is not about miracles. It's about being patient. Committing to a plan, and then wonderful things will happen.

The second secret of guerrilla marketing is to realize, in the pit of your stomach, when you sign your name to a check or purchase order or anything that is going to cost you anything, you are going to feel it's an expense, but it isn't really.

If it's marketing, it's an investment.

229

It's the best investment that is available in America today, if you do it right.

You're learning right now how to do it right because really the secrets of guerrilla marketing all end with the letters "ent."

One is *commitment*. The second is *investment*. The third is, you can't change around what you're doing. You've got to stick with what you started with, and be *consistent*. You can change your headlines, you can change the graphics, but don't change the media you're in and don't change the theme. Don't change your visual format. Don't change your overall identity. Be consistent.

The 4th "ent" word in guerrilla marketing is based on another fabulous study which was conducted in 1990 and again in 2000.

It had the same results.

The question they asked this time is, "why do people patronize the businesses that they do?"

Out of all the reasons, price came in 5th. Price is the 5th most important reason for a purchase. Just for a statistic, 14% of Americans have price as number one. That means 86% of Americans think there is something beyond "price".

The thing that came in 4th was "selection".

Why do people patronize businesses? "Service" came in 3rd. "Quality" came in 2nd

The overwhelming winner in this study was people said they tend to patronize businesses in which they are "confident".

Interesting how your commitment to a plan will make them confident. It's you hanging in there with your investment and not walking away from it that will make your prospect and customers confident. Your being *consistent* will make them *confident*.

The 5th "ent" word describes your personality. You are a patient person. Only patient people can practice commitment to hanging in there with an investment and be consistent enough to then make people confident.

The 6th "ent" word refers to the reality that with all the options of advertising, direct mail, the Internet, and other methods, what works best?
What really works is an assortment of weapons.

Ok, before we move into that area, what you're outlining, Jay, is that we are making that prospect, that customer, as you said, "feel comfortable doing business with us." Is that right?

Yes. That's it.
Make them confident in your business and in doing business with you.

Ok, Jay, we've got about eight to ten minutes to go. How about if I throw a few things out to you, we'll dance though it, we'll waltz through it. Sound good?

Sounds good to me.

Ok, this is advanced marketing 101. I am in awe. This is 18,000 times better than I thought it would be! I'm taking notes as fast as I can.
Ok Jay, the Internet is a huge business. We all know that.
Guerrilla marketing online, the Internet medium is an incredible medium for what we're talking about.
If I was someone just starting a website, I don't have the necessary huge funds, Jay Conrad Levinson, *Guerrilla Marketing's*, best selling author, what do I do? Where do I go?

I did a course called, *Guerrilla Marketing for the New Millennium* and its available from the same place you talked about before, Aesop.com.
That's the first place I'd go.
I say that because I wrote it for people who don't know anything about marketing but want to use marketing to grow a business. Or, they have a business and they want to make

it bigger and cut down the amount of money that they are investing in marketing.

All of the things that I'm saying, naturally, are in my books *Guerrilla Marketing*.

The course that I gave called, *Guerrilla Marketing for the New Millennium*, is up to the state of the moment. It's up to the state of what marketing is doing right now.

For people who really care a lot about the Internet, I'm sure hoping that's more and more people, I did another course called, *Put Your Internet Marketing On Steroids*. I did this course because so many people don't understand how they can save money on the Internet rather than how they can waste money on the Internet.

So, a course I wrote, *Put Your Internet Marketing On Steroids*, is also available from aesop.com.

They can go to marketingonsteroids.com as well and pick that up.

Talk about that. Steroidal marketing. I've read it.

Marketingonsteroids.com. It's a no brainer. Total no brainer.

Tell me about how do I put my internet marketing on steroids. A few tips in our remaining moments.

First of all, people must know marketing in order to market online successfully.

People who know nothing about marketing think they can go online and market successfully and it's going to be a major frustration for them.

You've got to understand marketing first, then you can market online successfully.

Another crucial thing to know is that it doesn't necessarily mean having a website.

Websites cost money.

You could market by using email, by joining forums and news groups where people talk about a topic that is connected with your line of business.

You can contribute information to this forum and you can get their names to email to them.

They are going to want to hear from you because you're on their wavelength.

You can join chat groups. There are many of them talking about your topic of interest.

Make valuable contributions. Get their names and email them because you know what's on their minds.

You can host conferences for a lot of Internet website owners. They are dying for contact.

If you can host a conference, they'll be happy to have you on. There are lots of sites out there that are dying for quality content.

Post articles on those. Write articles for these websites.

Charge them nothing, but have a paragraph at the end of your article that talks about your business. Include your phone number and how to get in touch with you.

It's going to cost you nothing. They are going to love you, cause you are giving them good content.

You'll be marketing aggressively. There's loads of sites that you can do this on.

There are lots of classified ad sites where it's absolutely free and you can even show graphics with classified ads these days and it costs you nothing.

Search engines are marvelous places. I agree with you aesop.com is the happening search engine right now. Search engines are another way where with the smart use of them, which is not going to cost you much money, is going to be a way for you to market aggressively online.

Now, notice, all these things I've mentioned: emails, forums, chats, hosting conferences, using classifieds, and search engines. None of these involve having a website.

It's all about what you are describing here, Jay, which I'm amazed at.

Guerrilla Marketing and the success of the series, the success of your students, the success of your website gmarketingcoach.com, it's really about going out there and doing it.

Forums, chat rooms, getting a list going, web sites, etc. It's about taking action. It's about following the mindset laid out and the personality traits and it's about sticking to the plan over time.

Exactly. That's on the button.

I think that's in your soul, Michael. I think it's what you're all about. I feel that you are an inherent guerrilla.

But, what you're hitting is the highlights of what we have been talking about or exactly what should be yellow highlighted in everybody's minds.

Talk about that power of that email list.

Is that something that we should really be focusing on these days?

One thing that you should not do is spam people.

Cyberspace is a new universe and when you send spam, you're littering it.

So guerrilla marketing does not ever believe in spam.

But, it does realize that you can get people's names by looking at newsgroups, forums, and chat rooms. You can get people's names and get their topic of interest and when you send them emails they are delighted.

Then It's not junk mail. It's not spamming.

I believe in targeted email. I believe in it like crazy. It's just like direct mail. Only without stamps and your subject line is the most important thing...

Say that again.

The subject line in your email is the single most important thing. Because people are besieged with 3,000 marketing messages every day and they make their decision lightening fast. They decide in three seconds whether or not they're going to read an email message, or listen to a commercial.

Therefore, it is crucial that you say something in that subject line that's going to hit your prospects between the eyes.

But you know how to do that because you know who they are. You're not sending out junk mail into the universe. You're sending out targeted emails to people where you know their interests.

If you do that you are going to find that emailing, targeted emailing, is very inexpensive, very effective.

It's growing like crazy right now, faster than ever.

That's because people are realizing that they can do it the right way.

I carefully select where I get the names of the people I am mailing to. They want to hear from me. They look forward to hearing from me and they want to buy what I am selling.

Then always lead with value, right, Jay?

Yeah, value is what people are buying.

They are also buying confidence in you. But, don't lead with price, because that's what most people think they should lead with. You're right, they are interested in value, not necessarily price.

So, one of the biggest mistakes business owners are making is they lead with price and coming from weakness.

Yes, and you know what happens when they lead with price? They attract the most disloyal kind of customers.

Say that again.

When you lead with price and lower your prices and advertise discount prices, you attract the worst kind of customers. Because they are disloyal and they are easily going to be "wooed" away by somebody else who's advertising a lower price than yours.

That's game you can't win. You just cannot win the game of discount prices.

Ok, Jay, we've talked about breakthrough after breakthrough after breakthrough. We've talked about the $25,000 marketing plan. I'm almost speechless for the first time in weeks.

We've got about a minute and a half left.

Jay, are there any other books from a mental, marketing, or business standpoint you can share with my audience? Any other books you can recommend?

I think the most important book I've written, beyond the books about guerrilla marketing or *Mastering Guerrilla Marketing* which is my newest book, is a book called *The Way of the Guerrilla*.

Because *The Way of the Guerrilla* has one of it's chapters about marketing, but all the other chapters are about other things that people living in the 21st century ought to be thinking about.

When I say that I work from home three days a week earning more than I ever did as a salaried executive at America's largest advertising agency, I'm thinking, 'anybody can do that.'

When I wrote *The Way of the Guerrilla*, it was showing people how they can put more balance in their lives, eliminate stress, not be a workaholic, and have a whole lot of fun because the destination isn't the end, it's the journey itself.

Jay Conrad Levinson, we're wrapping down the show. Jay, thank you very much for appearing on *The Mike Litman Show*.

Mike, it's sure been a pleasure. Thank you very much.

You're welcome.

A ton of hard-core marketing information. Can you take any, any more? See you next time on The Mike Litman Show!

236

FREE! - Two Special Bonus Gifts

As our way of saying *thank you* for taking an active role in your success education, we have made two additional bonus gifts available to you. They are each worth $19.95, and are yours free as a reader of Conversations with Millionaires.

All you have to do to get your bonus gifts is visit our special website at: www.cwmbook.com and the gifts are yours free. Thanks for reading.

Make Your Move
By Mike Litman

As you're reading this, you're life's getting shorter.
It's ticking away.

I'm not saying this to frighten you. Or even scare you.
Though it may.

I'm saying this to you to awaken you.
To inspire you.
To rise you out of you're deep slumber.
To really know you won't live forever.
To share your unique gifts.
To ignite your great inner fire.

To ignite your great inner strength.
To ignite your great inner light.
To shine. Brightly shine.
To ignite your great inner beauty.

To motivate. Yourself and others.
To love. Yourself and others.

To paint.
To write.
To teach.
To innovate.
To sing.
To dance.
To care.
To feel.
To listen.
To learn.
To laugh.

The clock's ticking. The world needs you.

Make your move.

238

"Who Else Wants To Hear the Actual LIVE Recordings of the *Conversations with Millionaires* Interviews?"

Check out all of the material CWM Publishing has to offer simply by visiting us online at:
http://www.cwmbook.com/products.html

Everything we offer comes with a full and complete, no questions asked, 100% satisfaction guarantee.

See you there!

Thanks for reading!

Mike Litman & Jason Oman

PS: You may also order additional copies of *Conversations with Millionaires* at this webpage as well. Again, the webpage to visit is:
http://www.cwmbook.com/products.html

About the Authors

Mike Litman

Radio host, public speaker, and entrepreneur, Mike Litman hosts the 'World's #1 Personal Development Radio Show', The Mike Litman Show, heard in Long Island, New York and online from his www.MikeLitman.com website.

He has been featured on TV and can be found speaking with incredible energy and passion to companies on the topics of living your wildest dreams, going the extra mile, and increasing your energy to increase your income.

Jason Oman

Entrepreneur, public speaker, and business owner, Jason Oman has dedicated his life to his passion of educating and inspiring people to create the best and most fulfilling life possible.

While still in his teens, he began researching money-making opportunities and attended his first life-changing seminar at the age of 17.

After starting his first business at 23 years old he did over one million dollars in business by the time he was 27.

During that time he appeared as a featured guest on a top TV infomercial called, "Creating Wealth", and then went on to become a guest on radio as well as becoming an author and public speaker.